LINCOLN
LIBRARY

April 2012   133.1

D0836302

Ghost Hunting
For Beginners

Photo By Rich Newman

About Rich Newman

Rich Newman (Tennessee) has been investigating the paranormal for over ten years and is the founder of the group Paranormal Inc. He is also a filmmaker whose first feature film, a documentary called *Ghosts of War*, will be released in 2011. His articles have appeared in *Haunted Times* and *Paranormal Underground*. Learn more about his investigations at www.paranormalincorporated.com.

To Write to the Author

If you wish to contact the author or would like more information about this book, please write to the author in care of Llewellyn Worldwide, and we will forward your request. Both the author and publisher appreciate hearing from you and learning of your enjoyment of this book and how it has helped you. Llewellyn Worldwide cannot guarantee that every letter written to the author can be answered, but all will be forwarded. Please write to:

Rich Newman
℅ Llewellyn Worldwide
2143 Wooddale Drive
Woodbury, MN 55125-2989

Please enclose a self-addressed stamped envelope for reply, or $1.00 to cover costs. If outside the USA, enclose an international postal reply coupon.

Ghost Hunting

For Beginners

Everything You Need to Know to Get Started

RICH NEWMAN

Llewellyn Publications
Woodbury, Minnesota

FIRST EDITION
First Printing, 2011

Book design by Bob Gaul
Cover art © Ghost: iStockphoto.com/Nina Shannon
  House: iStockphoto.com/Sean Nel
Cover design by Adrienne Zimiga
Editing by Ed Day
Interior Photos © Library of Congress,
  Paranormal Inc. & Rich Newman

Llewellyn Publications is a registered trademark of Llewellyn Worldwide Ltd.

Library of Congress Cataloging-in-Publication Data
Newman, Rich, 1968-
  Ghost hunting for beginners : everything you need to know to get started / Rich Newman. —1st ed.
    p. cm.
  Includes bibliographical references.
  ISBN 978-0-7387-2696-0
1. Ghosts—Research—Methodology. I. Title.
  BF1461.N495 2011
  133.1—dc23
                    2011021090

Llewellyn Worldwide Ltd. does not participate in, endorse, or have any authority or responsibility concerning private business transactions between our authors and the public.

All mail addressed to the author is forwarded, but the publisher cannot, unless specifically instructed by the author, give out an address or phone number.

Any Internet references contained in this work are current at publication time, but the publisher cannot guarantee that a specific location will continue to be maintained. Please refer to the publisher's website for links to authors' websites and other sources.

Llewellyn Publications
A Division of Llewellyn Worldwide Ltd.
2143 Wooddale Drive
Woodbury, MN 55125-2989
www.llewellyn.com

Printed in the United States of America

Other Books by Rich Newman

The Ghost Hunter's
Field Guide

contents

introduction

You are probably standing in the middle of a bookstore with this book in your hands and asking yourself, "Why should I buy THIS ghost hunting book?" With so many different investigation styles and authors to choose from, what makes *Ghost Hunting for Beginners* THE tome to purchase? Well, I'm glad you asked…

First off, this book was written with beginners in mind. Definitions are given, concepts are explained, and step-by-step instructions are included with every technique (even the more technical aspects of reviewing evidence and using various types of software). Over the years, I have worked with a lot of investigators who lack computer expertise (including co-members of Paranormal Inc.—my investigative group in

Memphis, Tennessee), so I understand the frustration that comes with learning how to properly use a lot of new gear and computer programs. Because of this, I have learned how to break down this information so that anyone can understand.

The second reason you should purchase this book and take it home with you (come on, the coffee is cheaper there anyway, right?) is the *approach* of this book. While it's perfectly fine to believe in psychics and/or a God in the Heavens, the best way to investigate the paranormal is with proven, scientific methods. Besides the fact that this is the only method that will allow you to present actual evidence to a client, your friends and family, or the paranormal community in general, it also doesn't require you to have any special abilities or beliefs. Learning the methods within this book will put you on the path of the true, objective investigator.

Though there are quite a few other reasons I could list to encourage you to add this book to your ghost hunter's tool chest, the best reason I can give you is this: experience. Everything written here has been field-tested numerous times. Everything. When I talk about my methods of interacting with a spirit, I have done them. The specific pieces of equipment covered in this book are in my cases of gear. Many years of investigations in places like the Lemp Mansion in St. Louis, Missouri, and the Crescent Hotel in Eureka Springs, Arkansas, have proven that these methods work. And they will work for you!

It's one thing to watch paranormal investigators on television or to read about a particular haunting in a book;

it's quite another to actually step into the middle of an investigation and to gather evidence on your own. But don't sweat it … you've got *Ghost Hunting for Beginners* in your kit, right? So let's get down to it and talk about ghosts …

one

Human Experience

I cannot but think that it would be a great step if mankind could familiarize themselves with the idea that they are spirits incorporated for a time in the flesh … What a man has made himself he will be; his state is the result of his past life, and his heaven or hell is in himself.

—*Catherine Crowe* (The Night Side of Nature, *1848*)

What are ghosts?

Pretty much as far back as written language goes, tales of spirits roaming the earth have been documented. And unlike other culturally centered phenomena (such as leprechauns in Ireland), ghosts are present in every religion, country, and history. And, interestingly, though many cultures may have unique, specific *types* of ghosts (such as the Japanese *buru buru* that's said to attach itself to your spine and make you shiver), most agree on the general disposition of these spectral entities, as well as the activity that occurs around them. So what are they?

Most believe that ghosts are the spirits of once-living human beings that are lingering here on earth—sometimes for their own reasons, sometimes whether they like it or not. But the definition doesn't end here. Other theories are out there. For some, ghosts are nothing more than memories that are recorded in the environment that some people can see and hear and others cannot. Another theory states that *all* spirits become ghosts, but only the strongest can manifest themselves for the living (this goes hand-in-hand with the idea that the entire planet is essentially haunted). Suffice it to say, there are a lot of different views concerning what ghosts are (and we'll discuss this in more depth later in this chapter).

What's important to remember is that one prevailing attitude underlies every theory regarding hauntings and spirits: the phenomenon is a naturally occurring event. To put it another way, nobody "out there" is creating ghosts or enslaving spirits to our mortal realm. The understanding that a ghost is a completely natural thing provides the basis for two fundamental ideas that make up the world of ghost hunting: we do not have to fear ghosts, and we can scientifically research them.

Popularity of the Paranormal

Unless you're part of the 0.25 percent of the U.S. population that hasn't been exposed to television, you've probably noticed that there are a lot of ghost-hunting programs on the air these days. And if you're interested in this subject, you have most likely heard the radio shows, seen the paranormal websites, and read a lot of the books as well. Though this subject has always been of interest, it appears to be at an all-time high. Why?

Many (including me) believe that the decline of popularity in organized religion has a lot to do with it. Since many churches have decided to rely on a doctrine that often defies logic and what's accepted by the general population as scientific fact, people are moving more and more toward alternate belief systems and ways to understand the afterlife and the nature of the human soul.

Another factor is the general acceptance of the subject these days. In the not-too-distant past, businesses were reluctant to have tales of their ghosts circulating—much less featured in books and television shows. That is not the case today. With "haunted tourism" at an all-time high, many of these hotels, restaurants, and museums now market their hauntings and use their paranormal activity as just another amenity for their guests. (Shameless plug: just check out my other book from Llewellyn Publishing, *The Ghost Hunter's Field Guide*, that lists over 1,000 such places).

Because of these two reasons, the formulaic ghost-hunting program has been born. Producers all over the country are lining up haunted businesses, throwing in a handful of paranormal investigators, and then following them around with cameras. While some of these shows can be quite entertaining, it's good to note up front that these programs have a primary function that doesn't have anything to do with typical ghost hunters: ratings.

Television programs must have an audience or they go away. Because of this, *something* has to happen on every show—even when it's simply a lot of "boo" type moments, investigators hearing things that we (the viewers) do not, and seeing things that the cameras seems to be just a little too slow swinging around to capture. Am I knocking these shows? Not at all. As I've said, they can be quite entertaining. But you may not want to base your investigative style on them.

Long before ghost hunters appeared on television, they were around doing their thing. Let's take a quick look at some of the more notorious paranormal investigators over the centuries.

Brief History of Ghost Hunting

Though many point to the early Spiritualists of the 1800s as the first paranormal investigators, they were essentially thrill-seekers. Like many people today, they would mistakenly refer to themselves as being "scientific" when they really just wanted to see a ghost. Many prominent scientists of the day, and even performers like Harry Houdini, took great enjoyment in exposing the frauds who would often capitalize on the emotions of grieving family members and loved ones with their hoaxes. During all this, however, there were some serious investigators. The first worth noting is Charles Fort.

Born in 1874, Fort's name is almost synonymous with paranormal activity. There's even a magazine named after him and his work called *Fortean Times* and a group that follows Fort's basic principles of investigation called the Fortean Society. Though he would often present his ideas in the form of a fictional novel, Charles often went to great lengths to research the paranormal—even sifting through the files of the British Museum and many prominent libraries for decades studying unexplained phenomena. His attention to research is something we can still learn from today.

Another notable, early ghost hunter was Harry Price (born in 1881). Though he was often ridiculed, he was catapulted into the paranormal spotlight when he investigated and wrote about the infamous Borley Rectory. A photographer from *Life* magazine once accompanied Price during his investigation there and managed to photograph a brick levitating in the air. The reputation of the photographer (David Scherman) added to the generally regarded authenticity of the photo, as well as the haunting, and made Price a well-known investigator. Like Harry Houdini, Price took great pleasure from exposing Spiritualist frauds and was the first person to use scientific equipment to measure paranormal activity.

The last investigator I'd like to detail here is Nandor Fodor. Born in 1895, Fodor would go on to be a celebrated parapsychologist and even work with mainstream scientists

Double exposure of Harry Houdini and Abraham Lincoln.
Courtesy Library of Congress.

like Sigmund Freud. Though he would take a serious hit to his reputation by supporting the authenticity of "Gef the Talking Mongoose," he is mostly remembered for being the foremost authority in the realms of poltergeists and mediums. He would go on to write numerous books about the paranormal—many of which are still available today.

Other investigators worth checking out include Guy Lyon Playfair, Loyd Auerbach, Hans Holzer, and Dr. William Roll. All of them have written about their investigations and methods, and have presented theories concerning the paranormal and parapsychology. It's because of pioneers like these that we today can also explore the unknown.

Types of Hauntings

If you were to eavesdrop on a typical conversation between ghost hunters, you would quickly learn that hauntings fall into three categories: Intelligent, Residual, and PK (also known as "human agent" hauntings or poltergeists). All three of these types involve humans and/or human spirits. There is a fourth category called Infestation, but since this involves a non-human entity, it is not considered a haunting (more on this later). Another thing you would learn from this conversation is that the type of haunting we usually think of when we discuss ghosts is the "intelligent" style.

Basically, an intelligent haunting involves spirits that are clearly interacting with the living. Whether the ghost is moving objects, speaking directly to residents of the location, or simply performing actions by request/demand, these are the hauntings that ghost hunters look for. Most believe that this type of haunting also can be remedied in some way. If a spirit is intelligent, he or she can be reasoned with. Sometimes simply asking this type of ghost to leave is enough—at other times, these spirits may need coaxing from a member of the clergy, etc. Either way, this is the type of haunting we usually read about in ghost stories.

A residual haunting, on the other hand, is something altogether different, though it can exhibit many of the same characteristics as the intelligent haunting. This type of haunting usually revolves around a moment in history—a moment that's seemingly doomed to be repeated over and over and over again. Usually this involves a traumatic event of some kind, such as a murder or sudden death.

At other times, a residual haunting can be something as simple as a woman crossing a room to her favorite area of a house. Either way, a residual haunting usually involves an apparition performing an act while completely ignoring the living around him/her. It can also be a particular sound that's repeated on a regular basis—such as a well-known haunted location in St. Louis, Missouri, where the sounds of a gun shot and a body falling down a set of stairs is heard on almost a nightly basis.

Closely related to the residual haunting is the theory of "time slip." Have you ever heard a ghost story that involved someone seeing a whole scene from the past, such as a crowd of people in period clothing walking down a road or a horse and carriage? Many paranormal investigators believe that these are examples of time slips. What the witness is seeing has nothing to do with ghosts. Instead, the person is seeing a moment in history either psychically or through a physical rift in time.

Do animal ghosts exist?

According to many paranormal investigators, yes. Though most animal spirits are thought to be residual in nature, the occasional intelligent animal entity is encountered—such as a ghostly cat that purrs when people are around.

The final major category of hauntings is called the PK haunting—or more commonly referred to as a poltergeist. PK is actually short for psychokinetic. Interestingly, almost every bit of activity associated with a poltergeist can also be associated with an intelligent haunting—and in many ways, a poltergeist *is* an intelligent haunting. What makes a PK haunting different from an intelligent haunt is that this type of entity seems to be able to tap into the life force or energy of a particular household member (usually a young boy or girl) to perform an unusually high amount of activity. Famous poltergeists are known for numerous objects flying through the air, loud voices/sounds, and seemingly violent actions.

Because a PK haunting revolves around a living being, many believe that the person is actually responsible for the haunting. Whether it's because of unconscious psychic ability or conscious manipulation of those around them, many PK cases are not hauntings at all. Ending a poltergeist is often as simple as fixing the psychological issues of the living within that home.

Repressed negative feelings, anxiety that stems from puberty, and even common, everyday anger can provide the energy necessary for this type of activity. In some cases, however, cutting off the entity from this energy is not enough.

There have been a lot of heavily documented poltergeist cases over the years. I highly recommend reading more about the Bell Witch, the Borley Rectory case, or even the details regarding the famous Enfield poltergeist to learn more about this particular type of haunting.

Non-Human Entities

Over the years, there have been other suggested types of ghosts as well—though a lot of them end up being in the realm of the non-human entity (such as "thought forms" or "elementals"). The most well-known type of non-human entity is, of course, what most people refer to as "demons"—though these spirits go by many different names all over the world.

We will discuss more about demons later in this chapter, but it's important to note at this point that non-human entities are treated differently than ghosts. Unlike a haunting, when a non-human presence is detected in a household, this type of activity is referred to as "infestation." Demonic infestation is not to be taken lightly and must be handled in its own way. But, again, we will cover this a bit later.

One of the more interesting haunting theories that has been put forth, though, involves what paranormal author Troy Taylor calls a "portal haunting."

Though portals are usually associated with cemeteries, Taylor (and other ghost hunters as well) believe that many of the famous hauntings over the centuries might have been a temporary portal connecting the living world with that of the dead. Through these portals the spirits of human beings (and sometimes non-human entities as well) can pass into our world and interact with us. If this theory is correct, it could explain why some places, such as cemeteries, can be haunted without an actual death ever having occurred there. Portals are often considered to be temporary hauntings, though, so if you come across one, you may want to perform an investigation in a hurry.

Ghost Story— Bethel Cumberland Cemetery

Over the years, I have heard of numerous supposedly haunted cemeteries. But because of the potential hazards involved with investigating such a location (such as encouraging other, irresponsible investigators to visit there as well), I tend to avoid them. But there are always exceptions…

When a local Memphis television station (WREG-TV) ran an article concerning the "ten most haunted" locations in and around Memphis, the Bethel Cumberland Cemetery was included in that list. Activity associated with the cemetery included dark, shadowy apparitions, inhuman growls heard by visitors, and even sightings of a strange creature that was said to have the body of a lion, the head of a dog, a wreath of coarse hair (like a mane), and glowing red eyes. Basically, all the ingredients for a portal haunting.

Being objective paranormal investigators, we (Paranormal Inc.) decided to set aside our rule of avoiding cemeteries and to visit Bethel Cumberland for an investigation. We talked to the caretaker and obtained permission to investigate the cemetery, then gathered our gear for what we thought could be an interesting evening. Once we actually arrived on the scene and began the investigation, though, it was clear that not much was actually happening. At least that's what we thought until an interesting event occurred…

A local police officer was issuing a ticket to a speeder on the road adjacent to the cemetery, so we were waiting for him to move on, when a strange sound emanated from just beyond the cemetery fence. It sounded like a low growl that slowly ramped up to a full force sound that was startling for a couple reasons. First off, it was completely unexpected. And, second, this was an event that supposedly preceded an appearance by the creature itself!

Locals claimed that this entity would suddenly appear and then charge the fence that surrounds the cemetery grounds. Prior to visiting the cemetery, we had speculated that this creature might be a wild boar; this type of act is something a boar is known for, and the animal matched the description to an extent. Now though, standing in the middle of the cemetery and hearing the sounds for ourselves, it was clear that this was no boar.

Once the police moved on, we took a cautious look around the area for any evidence of a creature or spirit. None were to be found. And, unfortunately, nothing else happened during our visit. When we reviewed our audio and video footage from Bethel Cumberland, we found a couple of interesting things. Somehow, the loud growling sounds weren't on any of our audio recorders, though you could clearly hear us responding to the event right after it happened.

Also, right after the police had moved on, one of our video cameras had captured a perfect ghost light bobbing through the headstones. This was not an "orb," but an actual ball of light that weaved through the trees, paused at one tombstone, and then changed directions before proceeding off camera. This light appeared just moments after we had heard the growling sound.

So do portal hauntings exist? It's entirely possible. As investigators, it's important that we keep an open mind and give new theories a chance. You never know what you're going to find!

Other Types of Paranormal Activity

Much like the idea that poltergeist activity can be the product of an overactive psychic mind, there are other phenomena that have more to do with the human condition and psyche than with a ghost. This type of phenomena includes having visions, near-death experiences, and experiencing "time slips" or psychic impressions.

A commonly reported experience that's often confused with hauntings (or worse) is known as "sleep paralysis." In this type of instance, an individual partially wakes up from deep sleep, but finds that his or her body is immobile. Because of this, the person becomes afraid and convinced that something unseen is in the room with them. This type of occurrence has been documented all over the world for centuries and is associated with events like "hagging" (the belief that an old hag would pin a person to the bed while sleeping and steal their life force) and succubi/incubi (demons thought to terrorize people in their bedrooms for sex). This is a natural occurrence, however, and it has nothing to do with the paranormal.

There are also various types of events that are seen while performing a ghost hunt (and while reviewing the evidence) that are often mistaken for the paranormal. These include strange mists that are often the result of changes in temperature and orbs of light that seemingly appear on a camera's viewfinder/LED screen that turn out to be bugs, bits of dust, or simple refractions of light. It is unfortunate that so many paranormal groups around the

`One of the more interest- ing theories regarding ghosts states that every place in the entire world is, in a sense, haunted.` *With billions of deaths occurring since the dawn of man, it is likely that almost any location can be associated with at least one of them. So, why don't we see ghosts everywhere? According to this theory, a haunting has more to do with the amount of energy/attention that's given to an entity than with the location itself. Test it for yourself: pick a random location, supply some energy/attention and see what happens…*

world have entire websites of "evidence" that are nothing more than these types of natural phenomena. Don't be one of them!

Religion, Demons, and Inhuman Entities

Any time the subject of religion comes up, there is debate. While this is true even around the dinner table, it is more so when it comes to hauntings. Most of the time, when a client believes they are being invaded by a non-human entity, they are simply mistaking the intent or nature of a ghost. For instance, if you were to see a door slam right beside you, followed by a scary-sounding yell, it would be easy to believe something "evil" was present. But this could be as simple as a ghost attempting to get your attention.

Unfortunately, though, this type of haunting does, on occasion, occur. Activity that's primarily associated with this type of entity includes horrible smells (feces, decay, etc.), growls, physical attacks (such as scratching and pushing), and "hot spots" (these are just like cold spots, but … well … hot). Without several of these types of things occurring, though, it's most likely that you are dealing with a hostile human spirit that's simply trying to rid themselves of human invaders or is trying to defend his/her territory. If you do come to the conclusion that something inhuman is going on, there are a couple things to keep in mind.

First off, your personal belief system and religion must be put aside. The only opinion that counts in this regard is the client's. If the people who live in a location are Catholic and you attempt to do a protestant "deliverance" or "clearing," you may offend them—or worse, they will not believe the ritual was successful. Because of this, any time you encounter a non-human haunting, it's better to enlist the help of clergy (preferably of the client's religion). Also, each religion/culture has its own idea of what constitutes an in-human entity; examples of such non-Christian spirits include Afrit, Dybbuk, Ikiryoh, Incubus/Succubus, Rakshasa, Tokolosh ... and each of these is handled differently.

Another time that religion may come into play is when you're dealing with spirits who may feel trapped in a location and want to move on. In this instance, it's important to know the religious background of the spirit if possible. If a ghost was a practicing Muslim when he/she was alive, doing a Christian blessing on the house will seem ineffectual to the ghost. This type of help will truly only work if the spirit *believes* in this type of help, so a little research regarding religion may come into play for some hauntings (and if you're able to identify who the ghost was when alive).

Going into a client's home and throwing around your own religious beliefs is arrogant, presumptuous, and usually ineffectual. Stick to the scientific method and respect the beliefs of the client/location at all times. A good example of a specific religion having an effect on a haunting involves the Catholic religion.

The Vatican's official exorcist, Gabriele Amorth, has stated that he believes all ghosts to actually be demons in disguise, and that they are simply appearing as friends and loved ones to gain the attention and confidence of the living. Catholics who follow Amorth agree with this position, so convincing them that a former owner of their home currently inhabits it with them will be impossible. If you just remember to leave religion to clergy and stick to your scientific guns while performing an investigation, you will be okay.

Ghost Story— Private Case in Missouri

Paranormal Inc. receives periodic e-mails from people wanting our assistance with a haunting— and on one occasion, the prospective clients were particularly dodgy about the details concerning their activity. According to the e-mail, a disembodied voice was often heard in the home and a stereo was turning itself off. This family just happened to be the acquaintance of one member of our investigative team, so we decided to help them out.

Once we arrived at the home, though, it was apparent that much more was going on. When we pressed them for more information about the haunting, the matron of the house burst into tears and admitted that their son (17 years old) had drowned in a pond behind their home the year before. She was now convinced he was there in the house and wanted "confirmation." Interestingly, there were Catholic statues all around the house, so she clearly didn't agree with the church's stance that all ghosts are demons. She also clearly stated that the family did not want to involve the clergy.

Giving her the benefit of the doubt, we did an investigation and found nothing that would point conclusively to the property being haunted. During the investigation, her husband admitted to us that she was receiving counseling for the death of their son and that she had had difficulty accepting his accident. At that point, we told both of them that we did not believe the home was haunted, though we would confirm this through the review of our audio and video footage (and there was, indeed, nothing there). I also urged her to lean on her church and her beliefs to help her with her grief. We then thanked them for their hospitality and ended our investigation.

Imagine the psychological damage that could have been done to that woman if we had hastily told her that their home was haunted! It would have undone a year of therapy and caused undue strife on the family. It is for this very reason that all investigators must respect a client's beliefs and to be professional and thorough with every case.

Of course, if you believe in the existence of demons, you probably also believe in the existence of God. So if it makes you feel more "protected" or comfortable to wear a religious medal or symbol while performing an investigation, do so. This can be done discreetly and may be just the thing to give you extra peace of mind while visiting a particularly scary location.

The last type of spirit I want to touch on is the particularly strange form of non-human entity known to the paranormal world as an "elemental." Certain belief systems (like the Wiccan religion) consider elementals to be the spirits of nature that are empowered with particular abilities. They are usually summoned during rituals, though they do appear naturally on occasion.

At times, when an outdoor location is thought to be haunted, people will attribute the activity to an elemental—though this is a pretty rare phenomenon. If you encounter a case attributed to such an entity, chances are you are dealing with a normal haunting and nothing special. Wiccan practitioners are available (though sometimes hard to find) if they are asked for or are needed and can be utilized much like any other member of clergy.

Of course, the danger with ALL inhuman entities concerns the concept of "possession."

Possession

It's interesting to note that most people associate the word "possession" with a bad connotation despite the fact that mediums have been allowing spirits to temporarily possess them and speak through them for over a hundred years. This was the bread and butter of the entire Spiritualist movement! There are also forms of possession that take place during religious rituals that involve a holy spirit or entity entering a human being. Despite all this, though, when most people hear the word possession, they think of the movie *The Exorcist.*

The now-famous case of a young boy's exorcism in St. Louis, Missouri, that was popularized in the movie was by no means the first of its kind in America—or certainly in the world. Throughout the centuries there have been hundreds of documented possession cases. Despite this, though, involuntary possession is a rare occurrence—and one that should be avoided by paranormal investigators.

If you are performing an investigation and someone claims to be coming under attack, remove that person from the premises. If the person happens to live at the location, ask them to leave during your visit and attempt to gather evidence as you would normally do. Then refer the family to a member of the clergy. Just keep in mind that quite often people think they are under attack when in reality they are simply frightened, paranoid, and/or experiencing a simple haunting.

For instance, if a client hears disembodied voices in his/her home, and believes that voice sounds "evil," he/she will begin to be afraid. Now add in a spirit that's trying to get some attention by slamming a door and touching people and panic can ensue. Try to avoid agreeing with a client when they bring up the subject of demons or possession and concentrate on performing a good investigation. Often, the truth will reveal itself and you can assuage the fears of the residents without calling in a priest, etc.

Never, ever try to perform an amateur exorcism, clearing, or deliverance. The people who live in the haunted home will doubt the effectiveness of the ritual, it will (generally) increase their trepidation in the home, and it can cause adverse psychological issues.

Theories about Hauntings

With so many things to think about concerning a haunting, it's only natural for people to ask, "Why do places become haunted?" There are a few different theories circulating the paranormal field concerning ghosts and why hauntings

Believe it or not, there are entire cities located around the world that are considered to be haunted! *One such city is Eureka Springs, Arkansas, the site of the infamous Crescent Hotel and Spa. Residents of this area will tell you that, because of the prevalence of limestone in the region and the running waters of the popular springs, the entire area is teeming with paranormal activity. Sometimes areas are thought to have an inordinate amount of hauntings due to their positions on "ley lines," mysterious alignments of spiritual locations. And this is not a unique occurrence. There are many of these towns scattered around the world.*

occur, but they generally fall in the realm of voluntary versus involuntary lingering.

Voluntary lingering suggests that the spirit had a choice in deciding to stay behind to haunt a location. Reasons for this include earthly attachment, wanting to watch over a family member, and so forth. This is the most commonly reported spirit. Because of this, many believe you can still coax an entity to leave a place and to "move on."

As for involuntary lingering, this concept usually involves an environmental factor that traps a spirit. Many believe that certain types of bedrock and stone (even when it's used in the construction of a place) can serve as the raw materials needed to "record" audio and video events. Because of this, most hauntings thought to be residual in nature occur in these types of locations—though intelligent spirits are sometimes associated with these kinds of sites as well.

Another popular theory regarding the involuntary lingering of a spirit involves trauma. Because a person may have passed away in a state of distress (sickness, mental illness, war, etc.), he or she may not have been aware that they died and may actually believe they are alive. It's thought that these types of spirits exist in a state of denial and may not want to understand that they are dead.

Regardless of whether an entity is present due to voluntary or involuntary reasons, though, both types of ghosts can exhibit the same types of paranormal activity.

Typical Haunted Activity

When you begin researching multiple haunted locations—or you are approached by various clients about their hauntings—you'll notice that there are similarities in the events that are reported. Generally speaking, most haunted activity can be broken down by the five human senses.

On the visual side, most people think of apparitions, though it's rare that these are ever seen (it's considered the Holy Grail of paranormal activity and some investigators work their entire lives to experience this just once). More often, bursts of light (referred to as ghost lights, sprite lights, etc.) or "shadow people" are seen. Another visual element to a haunting involves seeing objects move; things like doors opening/closing and items disappearing are commonly reported at haunted sites. But more common than any visual phenomena are reports of audible experiences.

The sounds of voices, knocks, moans, footsteps, and whispers are the most commonly reported paranormal activity. Sometimes these sounds can be heard "live" by investigators, but more often than not, these sounds are of such a low frequency and volume that our ears have great difficulty with them. These usually show up on audio recorders due to their increased range of "hearing." (For this reason, the best possible microphone should always be used with audio recording equipment—but we will talk more about this in chapter 3).

Of course, some audio is quite loud as well, such as the sound of a door slamming, knocks, and bangs. Even the occasional disembodied voice can be heard in real time.

Other paranormal activity includes hot and cold spots, phantom scents, and the feeling of something or someone touching them. Many will try to assign certain types of activity to specific types of hauntings (much like a doctor would attribute symptoms to a malady), but this should be avoided as it often limits the objectivity of an investigation.

Historic Case— Haunting in Genesee, Idaho

One of my favorite books growing up was *The Ghostly Register* by Arthur Myers. If you can still find a copy, the book makes for a great read and is full of unique haunted cases. In one of the book's stories, a building in Genesee, Idaho, was haunted by the ghosts of a rat, an old man, and a woman with dark hair who was seen floating above a sleeping visitor there.

This particular building dated back to the 1880s and was being used to store various items, including a collection of crystals and rocks. The residents of the building noticed that after they moved in, there were quite a few unexplainable events taking place, so they slowly started to believe they were haunted. Soon this escalated into the appearance of a spirit—an old man who threw a phantom object at one of the residents!

According to eyewitness accounts, numerous other ghosts were thought to be there as well—and the paranormal activity at the site would then go off the charts (with the sounds of footsteps and bangs being the most commonly reported experience). This case is just one example of what you can expect at a haunted location: the unexpected! With an open mind and a keen sense of observation an investigator can take a sight as strange as the spirit of a rat in stride.

One thing to keep in mind when you are documenting paranormal activity is to not assign descriptions of good or evil to an act—or even attempt to describe any intention. If you have enough occurrences of an act that you can trend this into a set of circumstances, that is altogether different. But oftentimes, people are too quick to label an entity as being mean, evil, or even good. Stick to your guns and perform the best, most objective investigation you can using the scientific methods and equipment at your disposal. That said, let's take a look at the investigative process.

The Investigation

With electricity . . . every time you rub resin against wool you invariably produce a recognized phenomenon; but with spiritualism you do not always get results, and so it cannot be regarded as a natural phenomenon.

—*Leo Tolstoy* (Anna Karenina, *1878*)

Preparing for an investigation can be a daunting task. Besides getting your gear together (as well as the other logistics involved), you will also have to mentally prepare for the possibility of encountering the paranormal. Of course, this is exactly what we, as investigators, want. Many believe it's sort of politically incorrect to admit the desire to meet up with a ghost, but the truth is that nobody would go into this field without wanting to find one!

That said, preparing for a night at a haunted location begins as soon as you have gotten your case. Most of you might, at this point, be more concerned with, "How do I get the case?" Rest assured, we will discuss this later in the book. Right now, let's just say you've gotten the case and now it's your mission to conduct a professional and thorough investigation. It should be mentioned at this point that ANY case you take on should be done WITH PERMISSION. Every place is owned by someone—and that person should give you permission to investigate on their property. But, hey, you're going to be a responsible investigator, right? So you will have permission.

It's best to approach a new haunted location in three stages: Pre-Investigation, Investigation, and Post-Investigation.

Pre-Investigation

The first and foremost thought in your mind as a new investigator should be, "How do I approach this case *professionally?*" In most fields, certain methodologies and techniques lend more to an individual being taken seriously than a certain attitude does. In the realm of the paranormal, though, it has everything to do with approach and results. Now, some of you reading this will ask, "Isn't that the same thing?" Nope. Let me explain…

In a field where everything is under scrutiny and hotly debated, all methodologies are given equal keel. Scientific groups get just as much business as those that prefer to utilize psychics. It's a matter of personal taste as to who an individual will contact for assistance. So, chances are, whatever method you prefer for an investigation, there will be people out there who agree with you. But one thing that all potential clients want is a professional approach.

Being Professional

Being professional means actually preparing in advance for an investigation rather than just showing up with some gear and buddies. It means concentrating on gathering evidence vs. giggling/laughing and cutting up with your group members. And it also means assuaging the concerns and fears of the property owners to bring about a resolution to their case. Though it's almost impossible to prepare in advance for the excitement (or fear) involved with an actual encounter, every other item I just mentioned can be managed. And it all starts with how you treat the client.

Though it should be a no-brainer, the obvious must be stated here: respect your clients and their locations! If you say you're going to be at their home at 5 p.m., then be there! If they tell you not to touch their antique collection of beer cans, then keep your paws off of them! For people to feel comfortable with strangers roaming about their home or business there has to be a measure of trust—and this can be easily lost, so tread carefully. Though you may not think so, another basic step to being professional is *looking* professional.

Think about it from the client's perspective: Let's say you have been experiencing scary voices and objects moving in your house. And you have a small child as well. You don't know what's happening and you're afraid for your family so you call your local paranormal group. Then they show up unkempt, unorganized, and they're all wearing black T-shirts emblazoned with a ghost that's straight out of a horror movie. How much confidence would you have in this organization?

At this point, some of you reading this will say, "But we will probably be going to cemeteries at first so there's nobody to worry about on cases like that." Wrong. Besides the numerous reasons to NOT investigate a cemetery (more on this later), somebody always owns a property. Whether it's the city, the county, or a private entity, ALL locations are governed by someone and they must be respected. It starts with always having permission to be in these areas and always leaving them exactly as you found them.

One last suggestion I have concerning respect is this: if you inform a client exactly what you plan to do, you will be able to do more! It's amazing what you can do and where you can go if you ask. Many times over the years I have visited a haunted hotel and been amazed by what they will allow me to do when I tell them what I want to do and ask them for permission. These are the cases that, when I post them in a book or on our website, other paranormal groups send me e-mails saying, "How did you get into that place? Nobody's ever gotten to investigate there!" I asked. That's how.

Now that you have resolved to be a professional investigator, let's talk about what should be the first step to every investigation: research.

Research Strategies

Of all the things that separate serious paranormal investigators from thrill-seekers, research is probably the greatest. For people who simply want to be "scared" and to "see a ghost," spending hours in a local library going through old newspaper records is the least appealing trip possible. For those of us that want answers, though, this is often the first step to any investigation.

Though the Internet can often be the first step in your research process, it can't be the *entire* process. Some Internet sources pride themselves on getting the facts straight concerning the history and paranormal activity of a location, but the vast majority of them will accept their "facts" from any source with no verification whatsoever. This makes for a lousy investigation and often just perpetuates the urban legends that are associated with a specific location.

Often the best Internet source for a location is that specific location's website (if they have one). Many bed and breakfasts, hotels, restaurants, etc., list their own history right on their sites. Some even include ghost stories and sightings that involve the place (with the popularity of the paranormal constantly on the rise, many have found marketing their haunting to be a good thing). But, again, this should only be your first stop. Getting out of the house and going to local sources will get you far more useful information.

The best sources for you will be the local library, historical societies, newspapers, and city hall. Since visiting even one of these places may mean hours of work, you may want to plan a separate visit just for this (or at least allow for a day of research prior to a night of investigation). Your first stop should be the library.

In addition to archiving local newspaper articles, librarians are skilled at pulling historical documents and often know a lot about local history. They may point you to sources that aren't listed anywhere (such as people in the community who may remember a specific event or an author who wrote about a certain place). I've discovered that a portable flatbed scanner is often invaluable during these trips as you can digitally archive everything you need and save money by not making copies at the library. Once you have all the info you can get at the library, you may consider some of the other mentioned stops.

If a newspaper was around during the heyday of the site you're investigating, they also archive their articles and may have something for you. Historical societies are usually run by historians that specialize in local history and often have an amazing amount of knowledge about any given house, hotel, or local property. And a town's city hall will have information regarding property transactions (great for seeing who owned a place during a specific time), birth and death records, and even marriage licenses. These sources will help you fill in any gaps that you may have about the history of a family or property.

Often, as you learn more about a specific event, location, or person, you will slowly begin to understand just how much of a ghost story is actually urban legend. Separating the myth from fact is one of the best things you can do prior to your investigation, as it will save you time investigating the wrong thing! For example, local legend may state that "Aunt Martha" haunts the old Miller place. If you discover there was no such person as an Aunt Martha, you can avoid hours of EVP work asking the nonexistent Martha questions.

Conversely, just because you have the complete history of a family and their property, it shouldn't affect your investigation to the point that you have tunnel vision. Let's say a property has always been in the Miller family; it would be easy to assume that a member of the Miller family must haunt the house. But what if there was a previous house at that location? Or maybe there was a significant battle there when the area was a grassy hill. The history of any location in the world is a long one—and you can bet we only know a small percentage of it.

Lastly, I want to touch on a different type of research—one that's more about the logistics of performing your investigation. This is usually done directly with the residents of a place. Before prepping for your visit, you will want to know whether or not a place has power, if they have any activity outside (where the weather may be a factor and you will have to rely on battery power), and what the temperature/weather typically is during the time you plan to visit (as this will affect your clothing, gear, etc.). Knowing all this will help you have a successful investigation.

Equipment Maintenance

It's amazing how often this step is overlooked by even seasoned investigators—myself included. Current technology dictates that much of the gear that we use (especially digital cameras, camcorders, and audio recorders) has to be charged up before use. Whether you make it one of the last steps you do after an investigation (plugging in your gear for a fresh charge can be done during your review of the data you've collected) or one of the first before heading out, make sure that all of your gear—as well as any additional chargeable batteries—are all good to go.

Of course there's also plenty of equipment that operates on good ole store-bought, single-use batteries, so stock up on the sizes that your team uses (usually AA, AAA, and 9 volt). There's a running joke in the paranormal community that batteries are "ghost bait" due to the fact that many devices/batteries end up inexplicably drained during an investigation. I have found this to be completely true,

Carry checklists of all your gear along on investigations. *It's a good way to make sure you have everything you need and also to make sure you leave the location with all of your equipment. There is a sample list you can use in Appendix A in the back of this book for this purpose.*

so don't just take enough batteries to fill your equipment—take enough so that you can power up all your gear several times. There's nothing worse than having some great activity going on all around you and suddenly having no batteries to put in your audio recorder to capture it all.

In addition to making sure you are all powered up for your investigation, you will also want to perform common-sense maintenance on your gear. This means cleaning off the lenses on your cameras (oftentimes "orbs" captured by people at haunted locations are nothing more than dust on the lens), dusting off and cleaning gear that's stationed outside, and even making sure your clothing can handle the environment.

When you dress for an investigation, dress logically! What's the temperature going to be? If you're outside, what's the weather supposed to be like? And make sure you wear items that will easily identify you to other team members and passersby. If you're all dressed in black and you're walking around in the background of a camera, it's easy to mistake you for a "shadow mass" or entity. Don't worry about looking cool and dressing all in black. Worry about being safe and conducting a good investigation.

Choosing Your Team

Deciding who to take along with you on your ghost adventures may be one of the most important decisions you make. Besides the fact that you want individuals who have the same paranormal belief system as you (What use is a psychic on your team if nobody else believes in psychics?), you will want to take along people that you trust implicitly. If a member of your team approaches you with an eyewitness account of a full-bodied apparition appearing in a certain location, there should be no doubt that what he or she is saying is true.

Because most people only have a handful of friends they trust in this capacity, many paranormal groups opt to keep their team small. My group, Paranormal Inc., is one of these teams. We only have three members—and the other two are my brother and a friend I have known for over twenty years! Another advantage to having a small group is the lower likelihood of contaminating your own audio/video footage. The fewer folk that you have tramping around a house, the less people you have to worry about keeping track of. Ideally, you should know where everyone is at all times by tagging your audio/video (more on this later) and keeping a log book during your investigation, but when you have a large number of people at an investigation, doing this is almost impossible.

Unfortunately, many paranormal groups go to extreme lengths to get as many "members" as they can. They do membership drives, constantly recruit, and often do open investigations that allow untrained individuals to wander throughout the location being investigated. What's the point of this? Evidence gathered during such an investigation cannot be taken seriously due to the high probability of contamination. If you are looking for a social club, then make your group a social club! There's no advantage (and numerous disadvantages) to having a massive paranormal group unless you're more concerned with selling merchandise to your "members" than you are with seriously investigating the unknown.

When you make your decisions concerning your team, consider making it as diverse as possible, too. Try to have at least one female member and one male member. Experience has taught me that sometimes certain entities have an easier time responding to a certain gender than another, so it's nice to be able to try different approaches.

Of course, many paranormal enthusiasts go another route as well. Since some people do not have any friends interested in the paranormal and don't want to join an existing group, many opt for investigating by themselves. This is perfectly acceptable, within reason. If you are going to a place with on-site workers and patrons (such as a hotel, B&B, restaurant), there should be no problem with you investigating on your own. Just watch your step while moving around in the dark and keep your cell phone in your pocket (though turned off so it doesn't interfere with your equipment).

I certainly do not advise doing an investigation at an outdoor location by yourself—there are simply too many factors beyond your control (wild animals, weather, terrain, etc.). There is also a practical reason to have at least one other investigator with you—if you see/hear a paranormal event taking place, it's nice to have that corroborating witness!

Interviews

One of the most important things you can do when you arrive at a haunted location is to conduct interviews with the clients/inhabitants. Some choose to do this by phone or even e-mail prior to visiting, but for most this is a logical first step when you arrive at the actual haunted place. To this end, try to interview everyone who has experienced anything out of the ordinary—and, if possible, record your interviews using an audio recorder. (Be courteous and ask permission first!). And as you interview them, you will want to concentrate on a few different talking points.

First off, make sure to get as much information as you can concerning the specific paranormal events that have taken place. Where and when did they happen? What was the duration of the event? And so on. With enough information, you may be able to identify patterns concerning the activity, which, in turn, will direct you to the locations that have the highest probability of turning up evidence for you to capture. Other key questions to also ask include:

1. How would you describe the paranormal events you are experiencing?

2. Are you frightened by the events that are taking place?

3. Have you noticed any strange, but seemingly natural problems recently? (Electrical, plumbing, etc.)

4. Do you believe in ghosts? Are you active in any church/religion?

5. What is the history of the location? (Concentrate on any traumatic events or deaths that may have taken place at the site.)

6. Are you currently taking any drugs, prescription or otherwise?

7. Have there been any recent traumatic events in the home?

This line of questioning should give you enough background information on the case to determine what, exactly, is going on, what has happened there in the past, and where you can expect something to occur during your visit. After you have finished up your interviews, you will then want to perform a walkthrough of the location.

Walkthrough

Besides giving you the layout of the property, the walkthrough will also provide you with the technical information you need to conduct a good investigation. You also will be surprised how many more memories are jogged when you're actually walking through a place; some people experience a lot at certain haunted sites so it makes sense that they may not be able to remember all of it while you are sitting at the kitchen table conducting an interview!

As you perform your walkthrough, you should make a rudimentary map of the location and make notes of special areas. There are four types of areas you will want to note:

1. Hot spots. These are specific locations where something of a paranormal nature has taken place. Whether it's disembodied voices, a person that was touched, or even an apparition, these are the places you will want to particularly pay attention to. As you mark these places on your map, you may want to assign a particular piece of equipment to that area—one that's appropriate to the experiences there. (i.e. if the owner has often heard the sounds of moans in the living room, consider placing an audio recorder there.)

2. Off limits areas. These are locations that the owners/clients do not want you to intrude upon. Respect their wishes! There are usually good reasons for not letting you into these places. If you go to a lot of hotels, restaurants, etc., you will encounter these spots quite often.

3. Trouble areas. These are places that may pose a unique challenge to your investigation. Examples of this are places where it may be dangerous to be at night (sharp corners, big steps, etc.), are close to an air conditioning unit (so the noise may pollute your audio), or are even extremely bright because of outside light sources you cannot control (so the use of some infrared equipment may be inadvisable).

4. Power sources. Since battery drainage is always a problem at investigations—sometimes because of paranormal interference, sometimes because they just went dead—it's always good to mark working power outlets. A lot of gear can be plugged into an electrical socket, and this should be taken advantage of whenever possible.

Besides logistics, the walkthrough can help you determine what is normal for the site. While you are making your way around the location and making notes on your map with the owner/client, you should have your other team members follow behind you to take base readings. Noting the average temperature and EMF (electromagnetic field) reading for each room will help you during the night to determine whether an encounter is natural or of a possible paranormal nature. This is also a great opportunity to inform the client of your intentions while you investigate. The more information they have concerning your methodologies, etc., the more at ease they will feel about having strangers there on their property.

You also can take some reference photos of each area as well; when you are back at home and performing a review of your evidence, it's sometimes helpful to be able to "see" the room once again. For instance, if you come across a photograph that seems to have a dark figure standing in a corner, you can go back to your reference photos to see if that entity was actually just a floor lamp!

Historic Case—
The Dagg Poltergeist

In 1889, Canadian farmer George Dagg found himself in the middle of a lot of strange phenomena. When he discovered large smears of feces across his home's walls and floors, he suspected his son Dean was to blame. Soon, though, it became apparent that this was not the case when the feces seemed to appear even when Dean was nowhere around. Then more types of activity began to take place: windows would suddenly explode, items would move by themselves, and spontaneous fires would break out about the house. Having checked off Dean as a suspect, George turned his attention to his adopted daughter Dinah when she reported seeing a strange man outside in a woodshed. A local investigator named Percy Woodstock was called in and the woodshed was staked out. Imagine their surprise when a male, disembodied voice suddenly declared, "I am the devil; I'll have you in my clutches; I'll break your neck."

The entity would then go on to plague the family for quite a long time—with Percy constantly investigating and documenting the phenomena. At one point, seventeen witnesses would simultaneously see stones flying through the air and an organ start playing by itself. (These witnesses all signed a statement to this effect). Dinah would report seeing the entity in three separate forms: a black dog, the devil, and an old man wearing white robes.

Eventually, the entity moved on and all activity stopped at the Dagg farm. But the question remains: What exactly haunted the Dagg family? Most refer to the case as a poltergeist, but many others believe the home was demonically infested since the spirit claimed to be the devil. Of course, the typical symptoms associated with many simple hauntings are present in this tale as well. This case is a great example of the ambiguity that sometimes comes with investigating the paranormal—as well as the fact that what is happening is sometimes decided by what you *believe* is happening.

Investigation

So you've gotten the interviews, you've made your walk-through, and now it's time to get the actual investigation under way. Before you turn out the lights, though, there are still a few things you will want to do, such as create a rally point, lay down some ground rules, and assign specific tasks to investigators.

The specifics of actually conducting the investigation and using gear properly will be discussed with a lot more detail in the following five chapters. Each of these chapters tackles a unique aspect of documenting and capturing paranormal activity. For now, let's talk about the use of a "live-monitoring station" or rally point during your investigation.

Rally Point
Simply put, this is the place you are going to stage all the gear. Ideally, it should be a central location close to a power

source so you can recharge anything that needs it. Since you will want to rotate investigators to different areas of a site over the course of an evening, this can be the place you rally every couple of hours. Doing this will allow your team to touch base concerning personal experiences and give everyone an opportunity to use different pieces of gear.

Since many paranormal groups like to use a Digital Video Recorder system with cameras, the rally point can also be the site for your "command central"—or as we like to call it, the Live Monitoring Station. The only difference in this scenario, though, is that you will probably want to keep a person stationed there to monitor the DVR throughout the evening. Even if you aren't running a DVR, you may have some audio, video, or environmental information being recorded live into a computer there. Either way, this area should be easy to get to and should be utilized by all the investigators. Having everyone rally at this spot every two hours can be one of the first ground rules you set.

Ground Rules

There are a few things you will want to get straight with your team prior to diving into an investigation. You will want to lay out some group rules and, of course, there will always be "house rules" that are dependent on the location.

House rules are pretty straightforward. These usually include measures that limit the team to certain areas, that prevent investigators from using any gear or methods that the owners have identified as undesirable, and that are made to keep everyone safe over the course of a visit. Group rules, on the other hand, are made so that all members will adhere to a certain standard over the course of an

investigation—a standard that should be desired by everyone present (otherwise, why are they in your group at all?).
Examples of group rules are:

1. Investigators work in pairs for safety and
   corroboration of eyewitness accounts.

2. Investigators must announce themselves
   when entering a new area so that they will
   not be confused with a paranormal event
   when reviewing audio from that area. (This
   is also known as "tagging.")

3. No provocation of spirits unless the investigation is going nowhere and it is approved
   by everyone.

4. No whispering (makes reviewers mistake
   your voice for EVPs).

5. Silence is golden. Only one person speaking
   at a time.

6. No perfume or cologne during investigations
   and no smoking (so that these scents will not
   be mistaken for paranormal activity).

7. The smallest possible team should be in any
   given area to avoid contamination of audio,
   video, or any detection device.

8. Be considerate and respectful of the property
   owners and your co-investigators.

9. Use trigger phrases to change investigation
   strategy (more on this later).

10. The goal is evidence, not experience.

Depending on the size and degree of knowledge your team possesses, more rules may be in order, but for the most part, the bulk of them will fall along these lines. The key is making sure that everyone KNOWS the rules and follows them. These are, of course, rules for when you are actually at the haunted site. There are more rules that your group should follow in general—such as having permission to be at a location, no children at investigations—and these should be addressed at some point as well. There are also some major points that should be made regarding your investigation strategy.

Neutral Approach

To me, one of the funniest things that paranormal enthusiasts often say is, "I'm a skeptic. I don't believe in the existence of ghosts." Oh, really? I have to disagree. Let me explain: I TRULY do not believe in the existence of leprechauns. I am 100 percent convinced that they do not exist. So, would I ever become a leprechaun hunter? No way. Paranormal investigators do not get into the field because they *don't* believe in ghosts. It's one of the great fallacies of the paranormal world that, to be taken more seriously, you have to pretend to be a hardcore skeptic.

Of course, the word "skeptic" is misconstrued as well—and this leads to a lot of the trouble with the use of the term. A true skeptic is open-minded; he or she acknowledges that they do not believe in a certain thing, but also concedes that this thing is in the realm of possibility. In this sense, we should all apply a certain degree of skepticism to individual cases. What I'm talking about is going into a case with a neutral approach.

Sometimes when you are researching a really good case (such as a well-known haunted location that gets a lot of press), the evidence concerning the haunting can be overwhelming. While this is good from the standpoint that there may be a high probability of something happening while you are there, it can cloud your judgment during your investigation. I'll give you an example...

Let's say you are in a haunted home that is now a living museum. Since this museum has been open, numerous employees and visitors have experienced the sounds of phantom footsteps and heard voices coming from empty rooms. Charged with this knowledge, you decide to concentrate your investigation in the areas where these things occur. If you were to hear a low-volume voice at some point, or footsteps coming from an empty area, it would be easy to jump to the conclusion that you are experiencing the same paranormal activity that the museum has often reported. If you remain neutral, however, and don't assume that this is corroborating evidence to the reports you have received, you may discover that the wall vents in certain rooms project sounds from other rooms and that the voices and footsteps you are hearing were simply investigators in other areas!

Not going into a location with a believer mindset is important—but not any more important than avoiding a debunker attitude! Nothing is more annoying to the owner of a haunted property than a group of "investigators" coming into THEIR home and summarily dismissing every personal experience they have ever had. You will be in a place for a few hours; they LIVE or work in this location and are there a lot more than you. Listen to their claims with a grain of salt, but don't dismiss them. If you spend all your precious time in a location concentrating on debunking every little sound and experience, you will have none left for gathering data and investigating.

Neutrality during an investigation also carries over to another area—do not assume that you already know WHO is haunting a location. Over the years, I have learned that most places like to believe that a certain person haunts them. Sometimes it is a famous person who was once there (there are several places that claim Abraham Lincoln); sometimes it's the most prominent person to have lived in a location. This is the stuff of ghost stories and legends and it can often be wishful thinking on the part of the client.

It's important to make no assumptions as to who is haunting a place. Keep your EVP questions gender-neutral (or at least attempt to speak to both sexes) and allow for the possibility that someone from a completely different period could be present. You'd be amazed at how many times I have been at an investigation that had been yielding very little evidence, but things suddenly started to happen when the line of questioning went in a non-typical direction. Hey, wouldn't you take it personally if people were constantly confusing who you were with somebody that wasn't there?

Evidence vs. Experience

While we all love having personal experiences—and, hopefully, you will have these while out in the field—in the end, evidence is the goal. It's often said that seeing a full-bodied apparition is the Holy Grail of ghost hunting, but as good as this is, it will not impress the owner of a haunted place. First off, they may have seen this same apparition numerous times, so they already know they have an apparition! Second, they don't really *know* you, so you could very well be lying. Third, simply relating a personal experience does nothing to actually help the client.

Because of this, our goal as paranormal investigators is to get evidence of a haunting, whether this is photographic, video, or audio. Capturing environmental data (cold spots, changes in barometric pressure, strange electromagnetic fields, etc.) is helpful for corroborating the appearance of the paranormal, but it in itself will never be regarded as evidence of a haunting.

Clients have their own reasons for wanting validation: to confirm that they are not insane (or mistaken), to hush naysayers, or simply to bolster their reputation. These are all perfectly fine. But to do this, they will need something they can actually show to disbelievers to sway their opinions. Oftentimes an investigator will look at one of their co-members and say something along the lines of, "I feel like something is in here." Imagine what the clients feel! There's nothing wrong with this, but without evidence to back up your feelings they should be dismissed as simply being imagination. After all, you are in a potentially haunted place in the dark!

Historic Case—
The Smurl Haunting

Long before it was dramatized in a book titled *The Haunted* (by author Robert Curran) and then portrayed in a movie of the same title, the Smurl Haunting of West Pittston, Pennsylvania, was simply another haunting. The case involved a duplex that was occupied by two generations of the Smurl family and activity that seemed to occur on both sides of the domicile. Famed investigators Ed and Lorraine Warren would take on the case, and though the home would exhibit many signs associated with a poltergeist or a simple haunting (such as footsteps, objects moving, phantom scents), they came to the conclusion that the Smurl family was experiencing strong demonic infestation.

Because of this, Father Robert F. McKenna was called upon to perform an exorcism—an act that brought no resolution to the case. Then, for inexplicable reasons, the Smurl family decided to go public with their haunting and more sordid details emerged from the case, including rape by the entity (something usually associated with a succubus or incubus) and seeing a black figure thought to be a demon. When it became known that a book, and even a movie, was in discussion, the press generally turned on the Smurl family and labeled them as frauds. This was exacerbated when they refused to take part in a controlled experiment to test their haunting.

In the end, all that was left from the entire case was a series of personal experiences. The Smurl family, of course, had the bulk of them. But others were put forth by the Warrens, Father McKenna, and other people who had visited the duplex. To this day, the case is hotly disputed and it is widely believed that the entire thing was faked. But what if it was a simple haunting? What if the investigators had concentrated more on getting audio/video/photographic evidence instead of getting press? If they had taken a scientific approach, we might all have a completely different opinion concerning the Smurl Haunting.

Your two-part goal as a paranormal investigator is to gather evidence of a haunting and to bring peace of mind (resolution) to your client. If you keep this in mind with everything you do, you will stay on the right track.

Performing Day Investigations

Perhaps one of the biggest misconceptions in the field of the paranormal is that ghosts must be hunted at night. This is despite the fact that almost every haunted site has reported incidents that occur during daylight hours. While it is true that some equipment needs the dark to be utilized properly (specifically cameras or camcorders that incorporate a form of night vision/infrared ability), there is usually a work-around. These will be discussed with great detail in their respective chapters (specifically the Video and Photography sections), but suffice it to say that you can perform a viable investigation during daylight hours.

But what about the "Witching Hour" or working in "Dead Time?" Nonsense. These are devices used by television shows, books, and movies to incite fear or suspense. Years of investigations have proven to me that you are just as likely to capture paranormal activity at 3 p.m. as you are at 3 a.m. Besides, there are some perks to performing a day investigation.

First of all, some places are open only during the day. These include state/national parks (such as battlefields that are considered haunted), museums, and even some restaurants. Your chances at securing permission to be in a national Civil War site afterhours are little to none. The government is simply not interested in a paranormal investigation. During the day, however, you will have almost free run of the entire park for a small fee.

As for museums and other public places, though there may be some additional challenges involved with capturing paranormal activity (other visitors, more traffic sounds, etc.), it is entirely possible to do a mini, covert investigation. By this, I do not mean going in without permission, EMF detectors blazing! But there's nothing wrong with purchasing a ticket to tour a haunted museum, then turning on an audio recorder to capture EVPs, and snapping infrared photos (something you can do during the day with a couple filters) as you make your way through the place. It can turn a dull afternoon at a historic site into a fun and rewarding trip. Also, don't be afraid of asking your tour guide or another museum employee about their haunting. Many of them will be eager to tell you of their own experiences and what they know about the ghosts there.

Documenting an Investigation

The first thing I do when kicking off an investigation is to place a notebook and pen at the rally point/live-monitoring station. Every time something of significance takes place (or anything worth noting happens), it is written down. Everyone investigating should do this—and all members of your group should have access to the journal.

If you perform a lot of investigations, or if a large amount of time goes by between your visit and finishing the review of all your evidence, it will be easy to forget a lot of the details. You may remember hearing a disembodied voice speak directly into your ear, but the strange, floating electromagnetic field that seemed to appear on occasion over a certain bed might be entirely forgotten.

Once you have completely finished reviewing all data from an investigation, you will be making a report back to the client. Your journal will be instrumental in making sure you do not forget anything that happened during your visit.

Setting up your journal is easy enough—and it can be as simple as a spiral notebook, or as nice as a leather-bound book. Start by writing down the specifics of the site: the address or directions to get back there, the date of your investigation (and time you were there), and any specific environmental data that may be pertinent (such as a storm or cold weather outside that could affect the interior conditions). When that is finished, you can then begin adding your notes. At the end of the investigation, draw a line at the bottom and write something like "End of Investigation." That way, your next case will not run onto the same set of notes.

Using a log book/journal is one of the most basic and time-tested techniques you can use in the field. It's also pleasantly low-tech and inexpensive, so there's no excuse for not doing it! This, along with the vigil, should always be done when kicking off an investigation.

Performing a Vigil

It's often said by ghost hunters that your single best piece of equipment is yourself. It's often said and it's often ignored. It is, however, completely true. Without getting into the actual chain of investigation you should use (this is covered in chapter 7: DICE), it's important to understand right off the bat that you will never be able to capture any paranormal evidence if you are not able to detect where it is happening! And the easiest way to know what's going on is to perform a vigil.

So, what is a vigil? Basically, it's stationing investigators in various locations throughout a site (don't just concentrate on the paranormal hot spots), then simply sitting and listening. It's important that everyone understands the concept of sound discipline during this act. No whispering, no walking, no moving, nothing. As you sit there in the silence, you will begin to notice things. Usually they are of a mundane nature: the ice maker in the kitchen makes a rattle when it kicks on, the heater makes a ticking sound when it heats up, etc. These sounds are important and should be noted in your journal. Again, when you are days (or even weeks or months) past the actual investigation, it is easy to forget those strange sounds when you are reviewing your audio.

In addition to the vigil, there are many low-tech approaches to ghost hunting. *Such techniques include the use of chalk or tape. Chalk and/or tape is great for marking the position of an item to monitor whether or not it has been moved over the course of an investigation. Just be sure to take "before" photos along with the "after" photos.*

On occasion, your vigil will also yield something a bit more interesting. A lot of parapsychologists currently believe that EVPs (electronic voice phenomena) are nothing more than disembodied voices captured at an extremely low volume, at an often hard-to-hear frequency. If you are performing a vigil correctly, you significantly increase your chances of hearing these ghostly voices in real time or catching other low-volume sounds (such as an object barely moving or light footsteps).

Using Walkies and Line-of-Sight

Since performing a thorough investigation can take some time, it's important for everyone in your group to stay in contact with each other. There are several ways to do this—and most of the time, the low-tech approach is best.

Staying in touch with your investigators can be as easy as having everyone meet at regular intervals at the rally point you have designated. This approach works for most everyone because you can also use these opportunities to allow everyone to switch locations to investigate (nobody wants to spend the entire night in one room or spot). It also allows people to get batteries, change out gear, and otherwise retool. Of course, if the haunted site is small enough, you may be able to keep all your investigators in "line-of-sight."

This just means you can actually see your other members in the next room, etc. This technique works well with small groups. Since you don't want to crowd everyone in one place, you can work individually in different rooms, provided you can still see another investigator in an adjoining area (with them that close, they can still respond quickly if activity starts happening around you).

Of course, a lot of paranormal groups opt to use walkie-talkies because they are now quite affordable. This can be a great tool for you provided people don't abuse them; carrying a walkie often breeds laziness on the part of investigators and you'll start hearing people using them to summon more batteries, hold a conversation, or some other unneccessary communication. Besides using up batteries, this is also bad because all the audio/video devices in the area are now being contaminated by the walkies!

Whichever method you choose to employ, stay up on what your co-investigators are doing. It will assist you with keying in on activity, keep everyone safe, and also help you to react quickly if something major goes down....

Reacting to an Encounter

It's interesting that all ghost hunters claim to want to see an apparition very badly. Interesting because almost everyone who has actually had such an encounter has pretty much been changed forever! When such an event occurs, different people will have different reactions. When I first saw such a spectacle, I reacted with excitement so intense that I was unable to get words out fast enough to my co-investigators. Another member of our group was so startled by the sight of an apparition that he jumped about two feet in the air and nearly tore off my shirt while trying to get my attention!

How will you react? There's no telling. The best you can do is to try to mentally prepare for such a sighting. Brief everyone on your team and try to set a standard for just such an occurrence:

1. Remain calm. Do your best not to scream or yell and try to get the closest investigator to you to corroborate the event.

2. If necessary, leave the area. Don't run or freak out (though this is easier said than done). Go outside or away from the investigation and calm down.

3. Document the event with as much detail as you can in the investigation journal and/or with an audio recorder. The more time that passes after your encounter, the more your mind will try to convince you that it didn't happen. You will begin to question even the biggest of details after a while.

Ghost Story— Magnolia Manor

As mentioned before, encountering an apparition can be a life-changing, if not terrifying, event. One particular encounter has always stuck with me over the years—and it serves as a great example for those out there who always wonder why nobody has ever captured a great video of an apparition materializing.

Our team was visiting a well-known haunted bed and breakfast in Bolivar, Tennessee, called Magnolia Manor. We were shooting a segment for the movie *Ghosts of War* (a documentary about haunted Civil War sites). We were setting up cameras—for both surveillance and production of the film—and generally trying to figure out how to get production footage of us ghost hunting while preserving the integrity of our actual investigation (a task that I do not envy with ongoing paranormal television programs).

According to the owners—and on-site residents—of the B&B, the apparition of an older woman had often been witnessed sitting in a rocking chair in the room we were working in. So we believed that our best shot of getting this act on camera was to place an investigation camcorder opposite the rocking chair and to focus the production camera on our team attempting to coax the female spirit into showing up. This went on for some time with no results, so as a last resort, we turned to mild provocation. We told the spirit (who was thought to be a protective previous owner of the property) that our equipment cases were suitcases and that we were "moving in" and taking over her house.

I did all this while sitting in the very chair the apparition was said to appear in (I thought this would also possibly instigate some activity). It was at this moment that I suddenly saw in the back corner—just behind the surveillance camera we had set up (naturally)—what looked like the upper torso and possible bald head of a man appearing! In great excitement, I leapt from the rocking chair and pointed at the corner. Everybody made a great attempt at swinging the production cameras in that direction, but the momentary glimpse of an apparition was gone. It was just that fast.

We would go on to rethink our approach and discuss repositioning the cameras, but the event would not repeat that evening. Interestingly, though, our audio recorders that were rolling in the room would go on to get several key EVPs. While provoking the female entity, you can clearly hear a female voice say, "I know it," when I say that I'm going to move in and change all the décor. And while we were discussing moving our surveillance camera to the opposite side of the room, we caught a male voice clearly say, "Put that sucker over there."

The bottom line is, though it would be great to capture video footage of an apparition, the likelihood of doing so is extremely low. Most of these events take place very quickly and putting your camera in the right place at the right time might prove impossible. So do not despair if you don't get this kind of evidence!

Post-Investigation

Whether you have reached the end of your allotted time for an investigation or the sun is starting to peek over the horizon, it's now time to wrap it all up. Once all the gear is all packed up, you will want to do a thorough walkthrough of the property to make sure you did not leave a camera, audio recorder, or other equipment left sitting anywhere. Since paranormal groups rarely make money performing an investigation (any windfall usually goes toward expenses), you don't also want to lose money replacing gear!

You will then let the client know that you are finished for the evening and give them a brief rundown of what is going to happen next. Give them a realistic time frame regarding the review of all the data you have collected and reassure them that they will get a copy of everything you have captured. This would also be a good time to discuss confidentiality—specifically, that you will not divulge any details about the investigation with anyone else until given permission.

You should also be careful about making any hasty declarations regarding whether the site is actually haunted or not. Besides the fact that your audio/video footage may prove a supposedly paranormal event to be of a mundane nature, you will not want to potentially upset the client.

Psychological Ramifications of a Haunting
It's important to always remember that, while you may find investigating the paranormal the most thrilling thing in the world, the client/resident may not. In fact, they may be downright terrified of what's happening around them. So, rather than making any kind of grand declaration of "being haunted," you should simply reassure them that you will

examine your data and help them out in any way you can. Since most evidence gathered from an investigation is usually discovered during the review, you should also be careful about making any statements regarding the location *not* being haunted.

It has always amazed me that there are actual paranormal groups that will "guarantee" that they will "get rid of your ghost." What?! How? Exactly how are you going to make a spirit leave a property? You can't make a ghost leave. Anyone who says they can do this is a religious wannabe who believes that ghosts are another form of demon and that they can simply be exorcised. Imagine what the poor client thinks when they invite such an investigator into their home because they have seen/heard a ghost and then that "investigator" tells them they have a demon there and an exorcism is warranted!

They will be terrified. And who could blame them? If they have children, there's a chance the trauma could cause permanent psychological damage. All because some so-called investigators have pushed their own religious beliefs onto a poor family who is simply looking for help with their haunting.

Conversely, a family that has been experiencing activity on a regular basis will become incensed if you inform them after a few hours of investigation that they are not haunted. As any reasonable paranormal investigator will tell you, ghosts do not come out and perform on demand. You can saturate a location with as many audio and video devices as you want and it will not guarantee that anything will happen. The highest probability you have at catching something will come from following the chain of investigation (DICE) and performing a careful review of your audio, video, and photographic footage.

Reviewing the Evidence

Though we will discuss in great detail the processes of working with your equipment in the next four chapters, it is important to note a few things at this juncture.

Once you have determined where you are going to perform your review, you will want to make sure your environment is as sterile as you can get it. By this, I mean that you will want no distractions and as few outside noises/sounds as possible. I also recommend getting a high-quality set of headphones to use while reviewing your audio and video—though you will want to avoid any headphones that have a "noise cancelling" feature since this can often cancel out EVPs along with the noise.

It is also a good idea to have as big a screen as possible for watching your video. I have seen people miss great pieces of evidence simply because they were reviewing their camcorder/DVR footage on their small computer screen (or worse, on the little flip-out screen on the camcorder itself). That said, your computer will be indispensible for your review. It will be on the computer that you extract small clips from your raw audio and video files, improve upon your photos and audio, and even type up your investigation report.

On the practical side, make sure you take regular breaks during your review to give your eyes and ears a break once in a while. Since you will be going over hours and hours of footage, it will be only too easy to get drowsy or to simply lose your focus. Since your best chance at getting any evidence will be in your review, you will do yourself a great injustice by not giving the process your complete attention. Once you have completed the lengthy process of review, you will now want to produce an investigation report.

Preparing an Investigation Report

Though this doesn't have to be extremely formal, it is always a good idea to put all your observations and findings down in writing. An investigation report is also a great way to note all the environmental factors during your visit (date, weather, who was present, etc.). This report will be good for several reasons: It gives the client something tangible when you are finished, it allows you to archive past investigation information, and it lets you trend information over the course of multiple investigations.

The first two reasons I just named are pretty self-evident, but let's take a look at the third … One of the biggest questions that seem to pop up on a regular basis is, "Why are some places haunted and others aren't?" Right behind that is, "What causes activity to only happen at certain times?" If you build a great relationship with a location, it is entirely conceivable that you will investigate there many times. My group has such a relationship with several haunted places. When you visit a site multiple times, you will begin to notice definite trends.

Sometimes this trend can be as simple as activity that seems to happen around one specific person (which is said to happen quite often with poltergeist cases). Sometimes it can be as complicated as certain combinations of barometric pressure and temperature feeding the activity (as thermal energy is thought by many to be a source of fuel for ghostly activity). By noting all this information in an investigation report, you can track it over time and use it to formulate theories regarding a specific haunting.

In addition to this information, you will also want to document the actual evidence (if any) that's found. Number the EVPs, video clips, photos, and other pieces of evidence and describe them in the report. Along with the report, you can then burn a blank disc with all the evidence (you can put an electronic version of your report on there as well). And if your actual evidence corresponds to the way you've numbered the evidence on the report (EVP 1, Photo 2, etc.), you will make it easy for the client to review the information later on.

Returning to the Location

So you've finished all of your review and you have your investigation report/evidence in hand. You will want to set up a meeting with the client to go over your findings. This is pretty much what you see going down in the paranormal television shows: the paranormal group discusses the investigation and shows what they found over the course of their visit.

As you go over the information, be sure everyone understands what you are showing them and that you aren't using too much ghost-hunting lingo. Not everyone understands what an EVP is! If anything you found is debunkable, you should attempt to do so. Let the resident know what you are doing and attempt to make sure you did not get a false piece of evidence.

If the location you investigated is private property (meaning somebody's home), you should reiterate the confidentiality of the case and respect the wishes of the homeowner. However, if you are investigating a public location, (such as a restaurant or hotel), you can ask the client if they mind if you post your investigation on your website or blog. Oftentimes, places thrive from their haunted reputation and gain a lot of tourism because of it, so they may actually encourage you to post your findings online. Either way, get their permission on an audio recorder or in writing and thank them.

After you have explained to the client why you believe their location is or isn't haunted, allow them to voice their concerns. Are they comfortable with what you have told them? Do they need more measures taken to feel safe in their home? They may decide they want a house blessing or another technique (incense, candles, etc.) to cleanse their environment. This is perfectly fine. Again, your MAIN goal is to give your client peace of mind, so set aside any beliefs that you have regarding clearing a house and oblige them. Call in clergy if necessary.

Specific Types of Evidence

When the investigation is completely finished, you can then write your article for your blog/website (if you're going to do one) and then archive your report and evidence. Some groups like to even archive the non-evidential footage from their investigation (we do so), though this can take up a lot of hard drive. If you want to go this route, you will want to pick up a dedicated external hard drive just for your archival information.

So now folks will go to your blog or website to read about your investigation and to check out your evidence. Notice that I just wrote "evidence." While your personal experiences can be an entertaining addition to your article—and most likely entertained you quite a bit while you were there—it is the validity and quality of your evidence that will separate you from ghost-hunting wannabes.

Evidence falls in the realm of four basic categories: audio, video, photography, and environmental data. The next four chapters will concentrate on how you approach each of these areas and how you will get quality evidence during your investigation.

three

Audio

I am a Spirit from everywhere, Heaven, Hell, the Earth; I am in the air, in houses, any place at any time, have been created millions of years; that is all I will tell you.

—*The Bell Witch* (Haunted People: The Story of the Poltergeist Down the Centuries, *H. Carrington and N. Fodor, 1953)*

If it weren't for audio recorders, most paranormal groups would never capture any evidence of a haunting. EVPs are the most commonly exhibited form of paranormal evidence and one of the most straightforward techniques you can learn. It's also interesting to note that the most commonly reported types of paranormal activity are audio-based, such as ghostly voices, footsteps, and knocks. But let's take a closer look at EVPs...

What is EVP?

Besides being the very reason the audio recorder is a staple for every ghost hunter in the world, EVP stands for "electronic voice phenomenon." In layman's terms, an EVP is a ghostly voice recorded on an audio device that human ears would not ordinarily pick up—similar to a dog whistle. Attempts at actually capturing spirit voices on audio go all the way back to inventor Thomas Edison, who claimed that he would one day build a machine for speaking with the dead. Of course, he never got around to building the device due to joining those he wanted to speak with.

After Edison made this statement, interest in communicating with spirits rose to the forefront of the Spiritualist movement. According to most researchers, the first successful recording of a spectral voice was actually accomplished by accident: filmmaker Friedrich Jurgensen was recording some footage of birds singing when he noticed a strange voice on the audio—a voice that resembled his dead mother. You can imagine his surprise when he heard that!

During the 1970s, a psychologist named Konstantin Raudive would record over 100,000 voices in empty rooms and other haunted locations. Readers of his work would dub the phenomenon as "Raudive Voices." Today, recording EVPs is an investigation standard—and, usually, your best chance of getting evidence at a location. So how, exactly, do we get EVPs?

The act of capturing spirit voices requires no special knowledge. It's usually as simple as firing up an audio recorder, asking questions to any ghosts that may be present, and then waiting a reasonable amount of time for a response. If you're at a truly haunted location—and you've asked the right questions (spirits are not required to answer)—you will, hopefully, have some great EVPs when you review your audio later on.

So, how do ghosts manage to speak without any vocal cords, tongues, or lips? Nobody knows for sure. There are a lot of different theories regarding the mechanics of EVP and how they are embedded into your recording device.

Thomas Edison and phonograph.
Courtesy Library of Congress.

Theories about EVP

So, if EVPs are the voices of the dead, how does an audio recorder capture them? Good question. Back in the days of analog-only tape recorders, many believed that spirits were somehow "psychically imprinting" their voices onto the magnetic coating of the tape. But when paranormal investigators turned to the world of digital media, and the ghostly voices were still being recorded, it quickly became apparent that this was not what was happening.

If there's no "magical" delivery method for getting the voices into the recordings, it stands to reason that audio recorders are simply recording audible sounds. Of course, the word "audible" is entirely subjective. Since most true EVPs are down in the low frequency range (sometimes as low as 3–12 Hz, which is interesting in itself since most people agree that human voices can only drop as low as 80 Hz or so), it's no wonder that ghost hunters rarely hear spirits talk in real time. Another reason for not hearing the voices live involves volume. Most EVPs are recorded at an extremely low volume—one that, as we get older, becomes harder and harder to discern.

Historic Case— The Philip Experiment

In the 1970s, the Toronto Society for Psychical Research conducted a unique experiment. They decided to go to a location with no history of haunted activity and to fabricate a make-believe ghost. They named the entity Philip Aylesford and gave him a backstory that included being knighted in England and serving in the American Civil War.

After several sessions involved with trying to "speak" to their non-spirit, things began to happen. According to reports, the table they would sit at would move, and they would get knocks in response to questions. It seemed that the newly arrived spirit was actually taking on the personality of Philip. Since this experiment, other paranormal groups have gone on to perform the same sort of test using EVP and have gotten interesting recordings.

Of course, this poses as many questions as it answers: Do ghosts lie? Or are they so anxious to speak to the living that they'll say whatever they think you want to hear? But, perhaps, the most pertinent question is, "Can ghosts be 'summoned' to places by the simple act of attempting to interact with them?" If this is the case, it sheds a whole new light on the very act of ghost hunting.

It's also interesting to note that science has proven that the human brain actually produces natural waves in the 3–12 Hz range. Perhaps the spirit still retains the ability to broadcast on these frequencies from beyond the grave ... At any rate, once in a great while, it does seem that the occasional ghost manages to have enough energy to get loud enough for our human ears to hear. These are known as "disembodied voices."

Disembodied Voices

Unlike EVPs, disembodied voices are heard in real time. This, of course, makes for a great experience when you are performing an investigation and is a great indicator that you are on the right track. (You'll learn more about this in the DICE section). When a client tells you that they hear voices in empty rooms, they are talking about disembodied voices.

Knowing the difference between an EVP and a disembodied voice is important. For a spirit to be heard in real time, that spirit has to have a certain degree of energy—energy that can also be used to manipulate objects or even to make the spirit actually materialize. Hearing a disembodied voice means that you now have the potential for significant paranormal activity—and can, in itself, substantiate a great deal of the reports a client is giving you.

If over the course of an investigation you actually hear a disembodied voice, you should note it on the audio recorder that's present. In other words, let's say you are in a parlor doing some EVP work and you suddenly hear a male voice speak from thin air. You should state right then that you heard the voice. This will help you when you are reviewing your audio to separate it from any EVPs you've caught (not that you're going to forget an experience like hearing a ghost speak!).

Historic Case— The Bell Witch

When it comes to disembodied voices, there's probably no case as infamous as that of the Bell Witch. In 1817, John and Lucy Bell owned a farm in Robertson, Tennessee, and lived there with their nine children. They all would witness and suffer poltergeist activity for over three years before the entity succeeded in killing John by poisoning.

In addition to the usual activity associated with poltergeists (objects moving, odd noises, etc.), the spirit who was called Kate (named after the recently deceased Kate Bates, a neighbor who held a grudge against the family after an unfavorable land deal) was also quite vocal. Her voice was heard by every member of the Bell family, as well as many outside witnesses, including General Andrew Jackson, who heard Kate taunt him after his wagon became stuck en route to the Bell farm.

Kate would curse at the Bell family, taunt them, and even make predictions regarding the future and her own eventual return to haunt the family at a later date. Activity, for the most part, ended with John's death—though while he was alive most of the attention was given to his daughter, Betsy. The Bell Witch is a great example of a disembodied voice exhibiting the necessary energy to perform a lot of activity—and it is why you should pay attention when they are heard during an investigation!

Along with EVP and disembodied voices, there is also one other way investigators manage to capture ghosts on audio: ITC.

Instrumental Transcommunication

Known throughout the paranormal community as ITC, instrumental transcommunication is closely related to EVP. The major difference is that, rather than recording the voices of the dead, ITC devices simply "channel" spirit voices so that they are heard in real time. This has been done in many different ways over the years and is still quite popular in the paranormal world (if a little more controversial).

The earliest attempt at doing this is also attributed to Thomas Edison and his "spirit device," though there's no proof that Edison ever actually created such a machine. In the 1970s, an engineer named Franz Seidl built a device he called the "psychophone." He would use it to speak to the dead for many years and even wrote a book about his experiences called *Registration of Supernatural Voices*. The aforementioned Raudive (an early pioneer of EVP) also dabbled with the psychophone and claimed it was an effective means for communicating with the dead.

Famed inventor Nikola Tesla also had a strange experience involving conversations with spirits. In the early 1900s, he constructed a rudimentary device that was similar to a radio but would create sounds as it encountered various electromagnetic waves. According to Tesla himself, strange things occurred when he used the device. He once stated, "The sounds I am listening to every night at first appear to be human voices conversing back and forth in a language I cannot understand. I find it difficult to imagine that I am actually hearing real voices from people not of this planet." Of course, reading this, Tesla may have been referring to the voices of aliens, not ghosts … Tesla's simple radio can still be made today and is now known as a Tesla Spirit Radio. Give that a whirl on Google …

Another famous ITC device was created by George Meek and William O'Neal in 1975. It is a variation of an AM/FM radio and is known as the Spiricom. Many researchers still use these units today—or at least a spin-off of them. One of these spin-offs is a modified radio that goes by the name of "Frank's Box" (named after the person who first created it, Frank Sumption).

The most common spin-off, however, is the "Radio Shack Hack," a simple Radio Shack portable radio that has been modified to constantly scan across the AM/FM frequency ranges. All of these are ITC-oriented devices—though radios do not always have to be modified to be used in the field.

The simplest common form of ITC, though, involves the use of "direct communication" through an AM radio. Those who use this technique believe that even though an AM radio can only go as low as 535 kHz, it may be possible to pick up stray harmonic frequencies that may be the dead speaking (this is a loose explanation for why a 3-12 Hz signal might come through an AM radio). With this method, you simply tune an AM radio down to the lowest frequency, and then begin asking questions. If you're lucky you may get a response through the radio.

I, personally, do not prescribe to using any of these techniques involving a radio. This is mostly because it is unlikely to catch a harmonic frequency so far off base (if a spirit's voice is even broadcast as

If you are interested in making your own version of the Spiricom or Frank's Box, you can find numerous tutorials on constructing a Radio Shack Hack radio on YouTube.

More information about George Meek's research and device can also be found on the website: www.worlditc.org.

a radio wave). Also, it is too easy to mistake a stray radio broadcast for a ghost—and many do just that! I still believe that to be a good researcher/investigator, all avenues should at least be explored, so if you decide to test direct communication through an AM radio or opt to construct a Radio Shack Hack, then at least scan the entire AM radio frequency range prior to conducting any experiments. If there are any radio stations in your area broadcasting, any experiment will most likely be tainted by the chance that station could be the source of your answers.

Like many practitioners of EVP, most who work with ITC believe that white noise (such as radio static) is one of the prime ingredients for capturing ghostly voices.

White Noise

You've seen the movie, now let's talk about the reality. Why do we use white noise and what, exactly, is it? There are a couple reasons for white noise making its way into the ghost-hunting toolbox; the first is that it is associated with the background static of a radio. Since AM radios were one of the first devices used to talk to the dead, many early EVP practitioners believed that this noise was necessary for capturing the voices of ghosts.

During the 1980s and '90s, parapsychologists used analog cassette recorders to capture EVPs, and it was believed that the natural noise that the mechanism made while turning the tape supplied enough white noise to facilitate EVP capture. Because of this, when digital audio recorders were initially introduced, many prominent ghost enthusiasts shunned the format. After all, digital audio recorders don't have any mechanisms moving to create any noise. It wasn't long, though, before people experimented with them and found that they could capture EVPs as well as, or even better than, their analog counterparts.

Today, there are still those out there who believe in the power of white noise. I am not one of those people. Research has shown that EVPs are as easily captured without the use of white noise as with it. In addition, white noise is NOISE. Noise that you will have to listen to when you are doing your review. Imagine sitting through twenty or so hours of steady static hiss! It doesn't make for a pleasant experience—and it makes sifting out EVPs a chore.

Curiously, investigators have also dabbled in other types of noise—pink and brown noises to be specific. They are similar to white noise, but are of a different sound frequency. Though I wouldn't make using any noise a staple in an investigation for the reasons I stated above, experimenting with things like this is one of the reasons exploring the paranormal is fun!

Now that we've exposed the truth of white noise—and know that it is nothing like it is portrayed in the movie of the same name—let's take a look at what we will need for performing our own EVP work.

EVP Gear Needed

During an investigation, you will need three things to perform an EVP session: a quality audio recorder, an external microphone, and a pair of headphones. Let's examine each of these in detail and explain their use.

When it comes to audio recorders, you will be faced with two formats. There are analog audio recorders, such as mini-cassette and cassette, and there are digital recorders. Though there are some excellent, high-quality analog recorders still on the market, I recommend going the digital route. Most digital recorders will feature a USB adapter that you can use to download your audio data directly to your computer for review (just check to make sure that feature is included on any recorder you purchase), which will save you hours of work. Without a USB adapter, you will have to play back your recorder in real time to get it uploaded to your computer.

Another consideration when browsing the audio recorder aisle is the format of the digital audio that is recorded. Recorders that come with a decent size of internal memory (1 GB or more) will usually have a recognizable audio format like MP3 or WAV, but economy recorders will often have their own, low-quality file format that will require you to convert your audio before playing it on your computer. These recorders come with their own conversion program which means there's one more step between making a recording and reviewing it!

A great way to get a good-quality digital recorder is to check out the models created for recording live music. They are a little more expensive, but they usually have a lot of memory, have a better built-in microphone, and record to a preferred file format. Sony, Olympus, Zoom, and Edirol all make this type of digital audio recorder and they can be easily purchased online.

Other features that you might want to look for in a recorder include whether or not the recorder is rechargeable vs. using only disposable batteries, if it also comes with a wall adapter (which prevents the recorder's batteries from being sucked dry during an investigation), and if it has "live monitoring" (more on this later). These features all add to the ease of performing EVP work and will increase the quality of your data.

Your second consideration for EVP gear involves the microphone. As I just mentioned, if you purchase a high-quality recorder designed for recording live music, you will most likely have a great microphone built right into the device. Most economy recorders, though, will require an external microphone. Since most microphone inputs for recorders are of a "stereo mic" style, you will want to make sure you purchase a microphone with just such an input.

There are two styles of external microphones you can purchase: a typical boom-style mic that can be held away from the recorder or a low-profile style mic that will essentially be flush against the recorder and simply look like part of the device. Most brands of audio recorders offer both types of microphone for their products, but you can shop around for the best deal since any stereo mic–style microphone will work.

One of the more recent fads in the paranormal world has been the use of gold-plated microphones, meaning that the diaphragm and (usually) the plug of the mic are made of gold. Many believe that gold conducts sound much better than the materials used on other microphones. This has not been substantiated, though, and the cost of such a microphone is significantly greater than a standard mic, so I recommend bypassing this until you have the extra cash to spend on experimenting.

The final item needed will be a great pair of head-phones. By great, I mean they should be comfortable, should naturally block out external noise (do not purchase headphones that have a noise-cancelling or noise-block-ing function, however), and have a large sound frequency range. When you look at the response of the headphones, the part of the frequency range that is important is the lower end. The lower the Hz listed, the better. Cheap head-phones may go only as low as 20 or 25 Hz. But for EVP purposes, you want to get as low as you can—if possible below 10 Hz.

There are many reasonably priced sets of headphones that go as low as 5 Hz, and if you spend a little more, you can even find those that drop down to 3 Hz. Many inves-tigators believe that EVPs are often vocalized in this fre-quency range (remember, human brains emit that 3–12 Hz range that could be associated with how a spirit speaks), so having the ability to hear these frequencies is important.

When you purchase your headphones, also take a look at the plug/adapter. If they don't have a mini-plug (that's the little 3.5 mm plug), you will want to purchase an adapter that will turn the ¼-inch plug on the headphones into a mini-plug since most microphone inputs on a com-puter and/or audio recorder are of this variety. Also, try on the headphones and make sure they fit. There are different styles of headphone speakers, so you will want to make sure they are comfortable, sit squarely against your ears, and that they block out external sound. (The over-the-ears style headphones that completely cover and surround your ears do the best job of this).

In addition to assisting you with a thorough review of your captured audio, high quality headphones may also help you with another, lesser-known investigative technique: live EVP.

Live EVP Methods

Simply put, live EVP is the method of actually listening to the audio that you are recording in real time. This means you can actually hear the sounds you are capturing on your audio recorder through a pair of headphones. And you will want to use headphones for this technique because playing the audio through speakers will cause feedback and will also pollute other audio recorders in the area.

There are two ways of doing a live EVP session: through certain types of audio recorders or through your computer. Since purchasing an audio recorder that already has this functionality is the low-tech approach to this technique, let's take a look at that first!

As I mentioned in the previous section, there are many digital audio recorders on the market that are geared toward recording live music. In addition to getting high-quality audio with the onboard microphone, these recorders often have the capability for live monitoring. Examples of this type of recorder include the Zoom H2/H4 and the Edirol R-09HR. In most cases, you simply need to plug your headphones into the recorder to utilize this function (though you should check your owner's manual for your recorder to make sure you don't have to adjust any settings to get live monitoring).

Want an inexpensive option for sound editing?

How about free? Audacity is an industry standard and features almost every option that more expensive audio editing programs have. You can download your free copy of Audacity at http://audacity. sourceforge.net/. Be sure to also download the Lame MP3 decoder on the same website to convert your edited audio back into an MP3 for easier listening.

If you are using a set of suggested headphones, you will (theoretically) be able to hear many of the voices you capture during EVP sessions live, during the investigation. The benefit of this is that you can hold a conversation of sorts. During a normal EVP session, if you were to ask, "What's your name?" You would have no idea if you actually got a response. If you were doing a live EVP session, you might actually hear a response, which would allow you to follow up with more questions—like, "What's your last name?"

Besides allowing you to have a more dynamic EVP session, using live EVP will also go a long way toward proving there is an intelligent spirit in your investigation site—especially if you're getting direct answers to questions that are posed.

If you don't want to spend the extra money on a music-oriented recorder, and you are already using a laptop computer during your investigation, you might consider using it for live EVP as well. To do so, you will need an audio-editing program that features a live-monitoring function and an external microphone.

While there are several such audio-editing programs, some programs cost more than a live-music recorder. Another drawback to using a computer is the lack of portability.

On the plus side, though, since you will also need an audio-editing program to perform your review of your audio footage, this may be something that you already own. You will just want to check the program itself to make sure it does have a live-monitoring function.

Direct Computer Recording

In order to use live EVP on your computer—or to simply record a regular EVP session on it—you will need a computer with an audio-editing program, an external microphone, and a pair of headphones (for live EVP sessions). Once you fire up your computer, start your audio-editing program and plug in your microphone. You may have to select your "input" as "microphone" to use the microphone jack in your computer (consult the manual for your particular program) and select "headphones" for your monitor to get it all working for you.

Hit "record" on the program and test the microphone; there should be a wave form that appears in the program and you should see a "level meter" that indicates there is sound coming into the computer. You may have to adjust the input volume in the program to get the microphone to a desired level—just make sure the sound being recorded isn't distorted. Hit the "stop" button on the program to stop the recording test.

Once you are sure the microphone is working, plug in your headphones and play back the test recording. Before you adjust any monitor volume in the program, make sure the volume on your computer is at a good level, then (if you still need the headphones louder) adjust the monitor volume. If all is well, you can delete the test recording and start a new recording for your investigation.

If you are going to go the live EVP route, make sure the live monitoring function is on and that you can hear yourself talking in your headphones when you start recording. Once you have your audio recorders and/or your computer up and running, you can then go to an area within the haunted location to begin an EVP session. (Don't forget to announce your presence when you enter a new room to "tag" the audio for review.)

Typical EVP Questions

The first thing you should do when beginning an EVP session is make sure there are no sounds present that can interfere with the quality of your audio. Though there will be some sounds that will be beyond your control (weather, traffic, etc.), you can do simple things like turn off any central heating/air conditioning units and place the recorders away from windows. Once the environment is the best it can be, begin your session by stating your name, your location, and the current time. You will be glad you started this practice after you have done a lot of investigations and the number of recordings pile up, because doing so will help avoid any mix-ups down the line.

Next, get comfortable and begin speaking in a normal voice. Don't whisper and don't speak any louder than you usually do. Whispering is a bad habit for paranormal investigators to adopt because a whispered human voice can sound like a low-volume spirit voice. There's nothing more disappointing than realizing your awesome EVP is actually a co-investigator whispering about something mundane.

While you are asking your EVP questions, you should follow a few guidelines:

1. Use the present tense. Instead of speaking to a spirit like they are dead and gone, speak to them just as you would another person.

2. Make no assumptions concerning who is present with you. I'm not speaking of your co-investigators here. Just because the legend of a particular site involves a young girl, it doesn't mean all your questions should focus on what a young girl would want to talk about. What if all the stories are wrong? If there's the spirit of a grown man present, and he is intelligent, he may be insulted by your line of questioning.

3. Try to keep the questions simple. Yes/no questions are best. Don't ask a lot of questions that require a long answer since it requires too much energy.

4. In addition to generic questions (What's your name? When were you born? etc.), ask questions that are specific to the location. Examples: Do you like the new paintings in the parlor? Is that you opening the bedroom closet?

5. Give enough time between questions for a response. Since it sometimes takes a while for a ghost to build up the requisite energy to communicate, take a reasonable amount of time between questions to allow for an answer. One to three minutes should suffice.

6. Try to speak one at a time. Sometimes multiple investigators will work in one area. Decide who will be doing the EVP questions, and then allow that one person to perform the session. When that person is done, someone else can take over. If multiple people speak, it can sometimes be hard to discern what is paranormal and what is simply an investigator when you're doing your review.

7. Avoid references to death and dying. In a lot of cases, spirits are not aware that they have passed on, or they are in a state of denial. Telling them something they don't want to hear won't encourage them to respond to you!

8. Use provocation as a last resort. Since there's no turning back once you've challenged an entity or insulted him/her, only go this route if you're getting absolutely nothing during your investigation.

Ghost Story—
Octagon Hall

It's always nice when your EVP sessions pay off in a big way. While we were investigating the notorious Octagon Hall in Franklin, Kentucky, my group performed an inordinate number of EVP sessions. This was because the director of the museum informed us that many groups had gotten great EVPs at that location in the past. In fact, he had heard so many EVPs from paranormal groups that he could recognize certain voices from specific areas of the house!

Armed with this information, along with a laundry list of hot spots in the building, we approached the investigation as newcomers. We would go to an area and ask any entity that was present to tell us who they were, why they were there, etc.

When we got back to Memphis, and went over the audio recordings, we were rewarded with several great EVPs. In a room where a young girl reportedly burned to death, we caught a young voice saying, "Help." The upstairs bedroom was the site of a ghostly, "You're not like me. I'm black." And after we had spent three hours working with the spirits there and had gone outside for a break, we recorded a female, "Hello?"

Paying attention to the information a client gives you is important; it can save you a lot of time investigating the wrong places and it can give you a head start toward capturing some great paranormal evidence.

In addition to working with ITC and EVP, there is one more audio strategy worth mentioning. There are several names for this technique, but the most common is Singapore Theory.

Using Singapore Theory

The basic premise behind Singapore Theory is that playing music from a particular era (that, presumably, of when a spirit was actually alive) will instigate a response on the part of the ghost. I can attest to the fact that this method does work on occasion. The only problem is that it makes assumptions as to who exactly is haunting a location—or at least what era that spirit lived in.

Once you have exhausted the normal EVP routes, though, there's nothing wrong with experimenting with techniques like Singapore Theory. The best way to try this approach is to once again integrate your laptop computer into the investigation. Since you will not want your music to be so loud that it drowns out any captured EVPs, using the tiny speakers on your laptop will work perfectly.

Since you do not know what particular era a spirit may be from, you will probably also want to keep a folder of MP3s that range across time. If you were to look in my Singapore Theory folder, you would find some classical music, some Civil War–era songs, jazz from the turn of the century, blues, and more.

What's really neat about Singapore Theory is that it can really get a spirit to sort of tune in to you and pay attention. This can pay off in ways that have nothing to do with audio, too. Since your audio recorders will be purposefully contaminated by the music, ask the spirit to do other things like move an object or knock on a wall.

Investigators have also used Singapore Theory along with other stimuli in order to facilitate a ghostly reaction, such as dressing in period costumes, using an antique item (such as a spinning wheel), or even speaking with antiquated words. By "re-creating" the environment the spirit was once comfortable in while alive, you may get the responses you want and capture some evidence of the haunting.

Whether you decide to use these approaches or not, once your investigation is completely over, you will have a lot of audio to review when you get home. Since a lot of audio recorders are reasonably priced these days, most paranormal investigators employ a handful of them during an investigation. Just think: 5 audio recorders x 5 hours of investigation = 25 hours of audio to review! And that's just the audio data. You will also have video, photos, etc.

So now you have all these recordings on your audio recorders, and they are sitting on your workstation back at home. What's next?

Analyzing Audio and Editing

For the sake of this book, I am going to use the free program Audacity to explain the process of reviewing and enhancing your audio. Almost every piece of audio-editing software will follow these same exact procedures—you just may have to consult your owner's manual to see how to do each step in your particular program. Again, I highly recommend Audacity for reviewing your audio, and since it is free, it can supplement any programs you may already own.

Okay, the first step in reviewing your audio is to get it from the recorders and into your computer. If you do not have a computer, this entire section will not apply to you; you will simply review your audio by playing your audio recorder and listening to the recordings through your high-quality headphones. Unfortunately, you will have no real means to extract a small clip of an EVP from the recorder. And if the recorder is digital, you will also have no way to archive your data since you will eventually erase your recordings to make room for new ones.

Again, for the sake of this step-by-step, I'm going to assume you have a computer loaded with Audacity. So you will want to start up your computer and then the program Audacity. If you are using an audio recorder that does not have a USB input, then you will have to use a 3.5-mm audio cable to connect your recorder's headphone jack to your computer's microphone jack. You will then select "microphone" as your input source in the program. If you hit the record button on Audacity, then the play button on your recorder, you should see your audio start to appear on the screen as a wave form.

If the sound is not being recorded into Audacity, make sure the volume on the audio recorder is loud enough (it should be set at about 80 percent volume strength) and that the input is correct (consult the downloadable Audacity manual if you need more details). If all is well, you will now have to let the audio recorder run until the end of the recording. Then hit the "stop" button on Audacity to stop the recording.

At this point you will want to use the "file" drop-down menu on the top toolbar of the program and select "save as" to save your audio recording to your computer. For medium-high quality, save your audio as an MP3 file. For great quality, select WAV. As you can see, getting your audio recordings into your computer using this method will take you quite a while. Hopefully, though, you followed my advice and purchased digital audio recorders with a USB adapter. Here's why:

If you have a USB enabled digital audio recorder, you will first want to connect your recorder to your computer with a USB cable. When the screen prompts you, open the folder to see the files in your recorder. You should be able to see your audio recordings as a series of MP3 or WAV files. Simply drag and drop them from the recorder folder onto your computer's desktop and *voila* they are uploaded to your computer! See how much easier that is?

Now rename your audio files so that you'll remember them (I usually label them with the name of the haunted location in numerical order, such as "Lemp Mansion 1") and open them up with Audacity. You will now see your audio as a wave form loaded in the program. Now that you have your recording in your audio editing program, it's time to review that audio.

Plug in your headphones and hit play in Audacity. You should now be listening to your audio recording. Adjust your headphones as needed—and keep in mind that most EVPs are extremely low in volume, so you will want to keep the volume pretty loud and keep your environment free of any competing sounds (turn off the TV, stereo, etc.). The controls in Audacity operate just like a CD/MP3 player, so feel free to fast forward, rewind, etc. as needed.

As you listen to your recordings, you should have either a pen and paper handy, or a blank word/notepad document open on your computer. Each time you notice a possible EVP, note the exact time of the incident with a brief description of what you heard. Once you are finished with the entire recording, you will want to scroll back to the times you noted and listen to each of those sections again. If you still believe the sound to be paranormal, you will want to extract that particular section as a clip.

To extract a section, you will go to the actual wave form and highlight just the section with the anomaly. Listen to your selection to make sure it contains the EVP/audio you want to extract, then go to the top toolbar and select "File" again to choose "Export Selection." It will prompt you to name your new clip (EVP1, etc.), let you choose a file format for the clip (MP3, WAV, etc.) and let you choose a place to save it on your computer.

You will repeat this process for every clip you wish to extract from the audio. Once you have pulled all your clips out of the main audio, you will now want to enhance your EVPs.

Enhancing Your Audio

Audio-production programs have lots of different tools for improving upon your audio quality. The problem is that many of these tools will actually alter your original recording—something that is generally frowned upon in the paranormal world. The more you tinker with your original recordings, the greater the chance you may accidentally change it, which could lead to false findings or leave good evidence open to dispute.

Generally speaking, there are only four "effects" that you will ever use in Audacity: amplify, noise reduction, low pass filter, and high pass filter. To use any of these, you will want to open up your EVP clip in Audacity, then under "Edit" choose "Select All" to highlight the entire clip. Then you can go to the "Effect" tab in the top toolbar and select the effect you want to apply.

Amplify is pretty self-explanatory and is a great way to increase the overall volume of your EVP. The noise reduction effect will help to pull things like rain, background hiss, etc. from your clip. For the bulk of your EVPs, these two audio effects will suffice.

As for the high and low pass filters, they are useful for isolating one sound and bringing it to the forefront. I advise experimenting with these effects to get the best sound you can get out of your EVPs. If you apply an effect that you do not like (or it decreases the quality of the recording), simply hit the "Undo" button to remove that effect. It's that simple. Once you've gotten the clip where you want it, save it and go on to the next.

It should be noted that, after you have enhanced a clip with any of the effects mentioned, you should save that clip as a new file. You can keep it the same name as the original clip, just make sure you note it as "enhanced" (example: Lemp EVP 1 Enhanced). That way, if you ever want to revisit the original clip to try new effects, you will still have it saved.

Once you are finished with the enhancing process, you should have all your EVP clips saved in a folder on your computer, ready to burn to a DVD-Rom or to share online. So, once again:

1. Upload your audio to your computer.

2. Review your audio in your editing program.

3. Note any EVPs or anomalies in the recordings.

4. Extract small clips of the EVPs and save them on your computer.

5. Open the individual clips in your editing program and enhance the quality.

6. Save the finished clips to your computer while preserving the original files.

Classes of Recorded EVP

Now that you've gotten your EVPs squared away from your investigation (if you caught any), let's take a look at the classifications of EVP recordings. The paranormal world has an extremely informal standard for labeling EVPs that's generally accepted by investigators. This standard has three classes of EVP recordings:

Class A: EVP is loud and perfectly clear. People in general agree what is said.

Class B: EVP is quiet, but audible and discernible with a little enhancement.

Class C: EVP is quiet and indistinguishable as to what is being said.

When paranormal groups post their findings online or share them with other investigators, they use these classes as a way to describe their audio clips. Capturing great Class A EVPs is a good beginning to any review and can go a long way toward proving the authenticity of a haunting. With any luck, the review of your video, photos, and environmental data will yield quality evidence as well. That said, let's take a look at the next thing you need to review: video.

four

Video

I now suspect that the spiritualists are reversedly right—
that there is a ghost-world—but that it is our existence—
that when spirits die they become human beings.

—*Charles Fort* (Wild Talents, *1932*)

Ahh ... the wonders of modern technology. With video cameras constantly becoming easier to use and getting higher definition—not to mention more and more features—it's no wonder that the camcorder has been elevated to one of the staples of a paranormal investigation. On top of all that, you add in the world of full-spectrum videography, thermal imaging, and night-vision technology, and you have a world of possibilities. Of course, you also have a world of dizzying choices, confusing formats, and hard decisions to make before slapping down hundreds of dollars on a video device.

Video for Ghost Hunting

The use of film cameras for chasing down ghosts goes practically back to the invention of the medium—though this would mostly involve still photography. Spiritualists, and the debunkers of the same, would often use photography as a means to support their claims. Motion pictures were only sporadically used because it was an expensive hobby for the time, and knowledge of these types of cameras was rare.

Once video came on the scene, though (along with the invention of television), the use of video at haunted locations would become more common. From the onset, early paranormal investigators would use cameras in conjunction with controlled environments in an attempt to capture spirits in the act of performing paranormal activity. But because of the low-resolution format and a lack of infrared equipment, the closest thing to evidence ever caught in the early days of video was the occasional "ghost light."

Today, the use of a video camera during an investigation is a must. Resolution is at an all-time high, the cost for quality cameras is down, and no special technical skills are necessary for most camcorders. Another key factor with the popularity of video cameras is the size—over the years, cameras have gotten consistently smaller and lighter, so keeping one in your gear bag is no problem.

Types of Video Cameras

When it comes down to it, there are three primary types of video devices: portable camcorders, wired DVR-based systems, and thermal-imaging cameras. Each comes with its own set of strengths and weaknesses, so you will have to determine your needs during an investigation in order to decide on the exact type(s) of camera to purchase.

Easily the most common type of video camera is the portable camcorder. In many ways, this is also the best type of camera to go with, mainly because of portability. It's always nice to be able to instantly pick up a camera and move it as needed. Also, accessories are easy to find—and you will be needing certain accessories to use a video camera effectively during an investigation.

Camcorders come in a lot of different styles: There are handheld versions (your common camcorder), there are palm-sized cameras (like the popular Flip Mino), and there are "prosumer" models that are typically large enough to require a tripod, but yield great footage. Generally speaking, these days almost every camcorder is probably going to be of reasonable quality, but there are a few considerations involved with choosing the right style.

First off, you will want to try to find a model that offers night-vision capability. There are numerous Sony camcorders that have this feature and a few Panasonic as well (and probably others if you want to take a good look around), so finding a camera with night vision is no problem. This function will be particularly useful for obvious reasons.

The next consideration will be how the video is actually recorded. There are tape-based camcorders that record to a Hi8 or Mini-DV tape and there are cameras that record to a built-in hard drive. If you already plan to edit video and review it on your computer, you will most likely want to get a hard-drive version. Besides not having to purchase tapes every time you use the camera, these cameras can often record uninterrupted for 8 to 10 hours, which is great for running surveillance on a specific spot for an evening. Imagine how angry you will be when you realize your camcorder ran out of tape when that apparition finally appeared!

Of course, if it's constant surveillance that you are after, you might consider buying a DVR system. These are security systems that are made for running for long periods of time and often include some sort of night-vision capability. Most systems come with a couple cameras and a hard-drive DVR (digital video recorder) that records the footage. There are several downfalls to this type of video system, though.

Because most DVR systems have cameras wired to the hard drive, they tend to have to be taped or secured in one spot, making them far from portable. Also, the wires themselves can be pretty intrusive at locations and can even trip you up during an investigation. For a lot of investigators, the final straw with DVR systems is that the camera resolution is usually quite low unless you spend multiple thousands of dollars.

As for the thermal-imaging cameras … well … let's just say the price usually puts them out of the realm of most beginning ghost hunters. A good thermal camera can run $10,000 and they usually don't even have the ability to record anything! If you use a thermal camera, you will also need to connect it to a portable video recorder to record the footage you are shooting. On top of that, using a thermal-imaging camera can be quite complicated because thermal energy often reflects off surfaces such as plastic, metal, glass, etc. This can make you chase a lot of false leads during an investigation.

Needed Accessories

Purchasing a video camera is usually just the first step to shooting good video. Since you will use your video camera in a lot of different situations, there will be some key accessories you will have to purchase. Here's a quick laundry list:

1. Tripod. Nothing beats a sturdy means to hold your camera still during shooting. Price and quality can vary, so I recommend trying tripods out in person instead of shopping online to find one that suits your needs.

2. Batteries. A lot of places that you will investigate will not have power—and some places will have it, but it just won't be anywhere near the camera! As a result, you will need several good batteries. These can actually be quite expensive, so if you're going to buy just one, get one that can last 6 to 8 hours.

3. Infrared illuminator/extender/light. They go by many names, but are the same thing. They're lights that make the night vision on your camcorder go much farther and see much clearer. Some run off their own batteries while some run off the camera itself (something that can drain your camcorder's batteries even faster), so take this into consideration when you purchase.

4. Cleaning kit. You must do maintenance on your camera to keep dust, moisture, etc., off the lens.

5. Video cables. Sometimes these come with the camera, sometimes they don't. You will want

to make sure you have a wall adapter and the means to connect your camera to your computer at the very least.

Other things like rain gear, equipment cases, etc., will come up, but if you start with the basics I've listed you should be fine for most investigations.

Using a Video Camera

Though most ghost-hunting shows on television feature investigators walking around with camcorders constantly in their hands, the best approach for most ghost hunters is to station your camcorders on tripods. In low-light situations, the video quality can drop considerably (which introduces more "noise" in the video footage that appears as a grainy picture), so you should avoid moving the camera around a lot. With adequate light, doing handheld work is a definite possibility, but if you are working in complete darkness using night-vision technology, handheld footage will often be blurry.

Another factor you may want to consider is the number of cameras you will have at your disposal. Since acquiring cameras of a reasonable quality will cost you quite a bit of money, you may only have one or two cameras total. This means you will probably want to put them in high probability hot spots around the haunted location. In addition to possibly capturing actual activity on camera (such as objects moving, an apparition appearing), you also can use a camcorder in conjunction with another piece of gear to document activity.

Let's say there is a particular chair that's known for cold spots. A good strategy for capturing this would be to place a digital thermometer on the chair, then use a camcorder to record any changes with the thermometer. Since paranormal activity seems to often happen in different forms concurrently, you also stand a good chance of catching visual phenomena. Other devices you can pair up with a camera include EMF (electromagnetic field) detectors, barometers, Geiger counters, ion counters, etc. But these are devices that we will learn more about in chapter 6: Environmental Monitoring.

Ghost Story—
Private Case in Tennessee

My group was investigating an Antebellum home just outside Memphis, Tennessee, that has a reputation for apparitions appearing to unsuspecting visitors. After interviewing the residents, we learned that one specific room seemed to have the bulk of the incidents. The only problem was that this room was massive, and it seemed that the spirit liked to pop up in almost every nook and cranny!

Since we knew we wanted a camcorder to be present in the room, it was tough deciding exactly where we wanted to place it. As we were discussing this problem, we noticed that a nightstand suddenly had an open door on it. When we had performed a walkthrough with the owner just a half hour earlier, it was closed. We even consulted the base photos we took during the walkthrough and were able to confirm this. Because of this activity, we decided to cover as much of the room as we could with the camera, but would focus it in the direction of the nightstand to see if the door would open once again.

Of course, the door never opened again. But if it had, there would have been a camcorder pointed at it. Sometimes you just have to go with your best odds when deciding where to concentrate your investigation and where to place your gear. Remember: ghosts don't always perform on demand, so the better the coverage you have, the better your odds of capturing the paranormal.

There are a couple of potential issues when using a video camera that you may want to pay attention to. First off, if you're going to use any kind of night-vision feature on a camera (and especially if you're going to use any additional infrared lights), you don't want to put the camera in a room with a lot of light, as this can blow out your video (give you an all white screen).

Secondly, you should think twice about putting multiple cameras in one room if you are using night vision because their built in infrared illuminators may actually shine into each other's lenses (but you can check this out by looking at the camera's viewfinder before starting to record). Also be aware that infrared light, even though it isn't seen by the naked eye, can reflect off shiny surfaces, so be careful where you aim your camcorders/infrared lights.

Another consideration is sound. Much like audio recorders, you won't want to place a video camera near any loud external sounds. Things like air conditioners, heaters, appliances, traffic, etc., can bleed into the audio track of your camera and make reviewing your video extremely tedious. It also keeps you from capturing any EVPs on your video camera (yes, you can do this). If you really want to up the sound quality on your video camera, also note that you can use a high-quality external microphone with your camcorder much like you would do with a digital audio recorder.

Using a Webcam

Since a lot of paranormal groups like to have a computer set up during their investigation as part of their "command central," many have started incorporating the use of a webcam. To do this, you will need your laptop computer, a good-quality webcam, and a video-editing program that can capture the footage coming in from the webcam. Essentially, when you are doing this, your computer is serving as your DVR. The biggest downfall to this is that most webcams have shoddy resolution at best—and little to none of them have any sort of night vision.

Once you have your own paranormal group, though, you may decide (at some point) to feature a live investigation over the Internet. This is entirely possible using a computer and webcam—instead of "chatting" with others over the Internet, you simply point the webcam in the direction of the investigators and now people who aren't at the location can watch your investigation and even join in by watching for paranormal activity!

Shooting in New Spectrums

If you keep up with trends in the ghost-hunting world, you probably have seen a lot more products on the market recently that cater toward shooting in "full spectrum." So what is full spectrum video?

In a nutshell, full spectrum simply means that you are shooting visible light (the things you see naturally) with the addition of infrared and ultraviolet light. Normally, we only see an extremely small portion of the IR/UV spectrum and since these types of light tend to spoil the look of photographs and video, most cameras are built with a "hot mirror" that blocks these types of light.

These days, though, there are a lot of paranormal investigators who believe that the low energy that makes up a ghost can best be seen in the IR or UV spectrum, so there are more and more full-spectrum cameras/camcorders being made. Usually these are just normal camcorders that have been hacked to have their hot mirror removed, but a few manufacturers make true full-spectrum cameras that are used for forensics work. (Fuji is well known for such cameras.)

Shooting in full spectrum can be a great way to explore new territory, though if you capture something in your video, you will have no idea what "spectrum" you actually caught the activity in since that type of cameras sees everything. In the end, it's probably better to shoot in one specific type of light at a time. At night, shooting in infrared is easy: this is what your night-vision camcorder is doing! Shooting in the ultraviolet range, though, is significantly more difficult.

To shoot in ultraviolet, you will need either a full-spectrum camera or a camera with night-vision capability. On a full-spectrum camera, you would simply add a UV-pass filter (check your camera for the specific size of filter it uses) over your lens and you will now be capturing only UV in your footage—the filter allows only UV rays to pass through. Filters screw directly onto the front of camcorders, right over the lens.

On a night-vision camera, you would add the same filter, and then turn the camera's night-vision function on. During the day, shooting in UV is easy; the sun naturally provides a ton of this. You'll even be able to see a nice, purple tint to your footage that confirms that you are shooting in ultraviolet.

Shooting UV at night, however, is a huge undertaking because you have to provide all the UV light. And it will have to be enough to produce a visible image after passing through your camera's UV-pass filter (a filter that looks like it is almost black). To make things even more complicated, there are several different types of UV lights available for purchase (plant/grow lights, reptile lights, sunlamp bulbs, etc.) that are quite often harmful to human beings. Remember, UV light is to blame for a lot of eye problems, sunburns, skin cancer, and the like.

The easiest and most economical way of boosting the UV spectrum is to purchase some high-wattage "black light" bulbs. Only these have any real chance of illuminating an area enough to produce a viewable camera image. That said, I would stick to IR or full spectrum videography during the night hours and leave pure UV camera work for daytime use.

When you are shopping for camcorders, pay attention to the features. *A lot of video cameras actually have the ability to shoot digital photos in addition to shooting video. Since you will want to take infrared photos in addition to shooting infrared video, this is a great way to get two pieces of gear with one purchase.*

You should also know that you can shoot video in infrared during daylight hours as well. For this, you will need an IR-pass filter (again, check your filter size before making your purchase) and, most likely, a neutral-density filter. Also known as ND filters, this type of filter is designed to knock down the amount of light that's going into your camera. They come in several different degrees of darkness (numbered .1 to .9) so if you are going to get just one, aim for a .5 ND filter. These filters are reasonably priced, though, so consider getting a couple ND filters (one low, one high).

To use your IR-pass filter and night-vision camcorder in the daytime, simply put on the IR/ND filters, and then turn on the night-vision function. You will notice that the leaves, grass, etc., are now a weird white color and that the sky seems almost black. Make sure your IR-pass filter is on the camera before turning it to night vision, though, or you risk damaging your camcorder's sensor.

If you look at your video image and it seems to be "blown out" or pale, simply add a higher number

ND filter on top of the IR-pass filter and the image should get darker and more detailed. Over the years, some great ghost photographs have been captured using infrared photography during the day, so this is a great tool to use.

Video ITC

Another interesting trend involving the use of video cameras is the sudden popularity of "video ITC." Much like the audio methods of ITC (Instrumental Transcommunication, see page 75 for more), this technique involves the use of "noise" to convey a message between a spirit and the living. There are a couple different ways to perform video ITC, but the most common/popular involves the use of a camcorder with a television set.

In this method, you connect your camcorder directly to the "Video In" of your television set, and then turn on your camcorder. You will notice that the television now shows what your video camera is "seeing." Now, position the camera so that it is shooting the actual television image. There will be a "loop" of the camera looking at itself, over and over again. This is called the "video loop" method of ITC. If you move the camera a bit closer to the television screen, you will eventually get a bit of feedback in the image/audio as well. This is a variation on the loop method that is often called the "feedback loop."

You can even turn a television on to a channel that has no programming so that you have a screen of constant static/ white noise. Now record that static using a VCR/DVR. This is another form of video ITC. In all cases, you are basically looking and listening for anything untoward in the footage

Alternate-Reality Theory is one possible explanation for the success some people have with video ITC. *According to this theory, there are many "planes of existence" and we are simply living on one of them. Tuning into these alternate realities is one of the reasons people use video ITC.*

that may indicate a paranormal presence. Many paranormal enthusiasts who work with video ITC prefer to use the "Klaus Schreiber Method."

In this version, you simply turn off the auto focus on your camcorder and, after you have pointed the camcorder at the television, adjust the focus so that it is slightly out of focus. (A good method for this is to point the camera at the wall behind the TV, allow the camera to focus, then turn off the autofocus and point the camera back at the TV). You should have an image that's sort of cloudy. Practitioners of this method claim to see apparitions in the video footage.

Unfortunately, a lot of people use this technique and then claim to see faces or images within the television static. This is a common phenomena that's referred to as "matrixing"—the tendency of the human mind to try to make sense out of nothing—or, as the scientific community calls it, *pareidolia* or *apophenia*. This misconception also happens with photographs as well. You will have to experiment with this technique on your own to decide if it's for you. You can also try other methods of recording noise as well, such as pointing a video camera at a pool of water and creating a small wave to look for images. (This is sometimes done with a strobe light added as well).

Historic Case—
The Amityville Horror

Of all the hauntings ever documented, none are as well known as the famous Amityville Horror. The Lutz family would report enduring a month of elevated paranormal activity that would eventually drive them from their home and spawn a whole slew of books and movies.

Over the years, there have been many different theories put forward as to why this particular house was haunted—sometimes by well-known investigators like Hans Holzer and the Warrens. Theories include the property being inhabited by the spirits of the dead (Ronald DeFeo murdered his family in the house), the presence of a demonic force, and even the possibility of the home residing on a Native American burial site.

One of the more interesting details from the case that came forward was a bit of video ITC that Ronald DeFeo later claimed to experience in the home. According to him, he was watching a television program in the basement of the house (a movie called *Castle Keep*), when whispered voices spoke through the static on the TV screen—voices that sounded like members of his family. The voices seemed to be plotting against DeFeo. A "figure with black hands" then, reportedly, appeared and handed a gun to DeFeo.

Opinions have always varied concerning the validity of the Amityville Horror story—and this bit of the tale adds to the controversy that surrounds it. It's also a great reason why controversial methods should be avoided when you are already researching a controversial subject like ghosts! Look at it this way: It's hard enough convincing the average person that a place is haunted. Now imagine convincing them of this by saying your evidence comes from television static…

Whether you decide to use video ITC during your investigations or not, by the end of a typical investigation of a haunted location, you will have a considerable amount of video footage to review and analyze.

Analyzing and Editing Video

The process of reviewing, uploading, and editing your video footage is quite similar to that for audio recordings—though the learning curve involved with mastering a video non-linear editing system (NLE as we'll call it) can be quite steep. For our purposes, however, we will only have to delve into the basics of video editing.

Most computers actually come with a basic version of an NLE installed these days (Windows Movie Maker on Windows-based systems, iMovie on Apple) that should work just fine for all the basic applications you will use. If you decide to step up to a program with more advanced features, shop carefully. There are many programs out there, and some can cost hundreds of dollars. You will also want to check out the "required specifications" needed from your computer for these programs. Some NLE's require a fast processor, lots of RAM, and specific audio/video cards in order to function.

Before you edit your video, you will want to decide how to review the footage you've captured. I recommend using the biggest screen at your disposal, which will most likely be your television set. Most camcorders have a "Video Out" port that you can connect to one of your television inputs, just check to see what kind of cable you will need to do this (USB, RCA, HDMI, etc.). The good thing about reviewing this way is that you can run your camera just like a DVD player and easily rewind as needed.

As you review the video you captured during your investigation, you will want to keep paper and pen handy to note the time of any anomaly. By this, I mean the time on the tape/hard drive as the footage is playing. It should be running

If you are using a computer without free video-editing software pre-installed, there are other alternatives. *A quick Internet search will bring you several free video editing programs like Wax and Zwei-Stein. Also, most NLE programs for purchase will allow you to download and run a trial version of the program for free. This is a great way to test a program before purchasing it.*

on the camera's little video screen or in the viewfinder. You won't want the time constantly displayed on the television because it could potentially block a piece of evidence from being seen.

Once you have finished reviewing all of your video, it is time to upload the footage to your computer for editing. To do this, you will want to start your computer's NLE and then use the "Import" function to get your video footage into the computer. Most editing systems do this the same way: you will be prompted to connect your camcorder to your computer, then you can fast forward (or rewind) to each of the times you noted something paranormal.

Once you are at the moment you want to upload, hit "Record" on the NLE and you will be uploading your footage. If you hit any snags getting this to work, consult the manual or "Help" function in your NLE. When the clip is finished uploading, hit "Stop" on the NLE and the program will prompt you to save the video clip as a file. Save the file, close it, and go on to the next clip. Repeat as necessary.

As with your audio clips, there are quite a few video file formats to choose from. I recommend saving your clips in both a low-resolution format and a high-resolution format. Low-resolution formats include FLV and WMV files. These will be the clips that you will post online and share. High resolution formats include MP4 and MOV files. These are the clips you can watch at home, archive, etc.

On the "enhancing" front for video, there's not a lot that you will want to do. If the video is too dark, you can usually lighten it without too much trouble (again, consult your NLE's manual for instructions) and the volume of the audio can be increased without difficulty as well. For the most part, this is all you should do to any video you've captured. More than this and you open yourself (and your evidence) up to accusations of tampering with the footage. A lot of the effects that are included with NLE systems (such as "contrast" and "correction" functions) can often create odd video artifacts that can be confused with paranormal activity and change the appearance of the objects in frame.

Now that we've covered capturing, reviewing, and editing audio and video, it's time to move on to the next major category of evidence: photography.

Photography

We must stop asking: Can these things be? And begin asking: Why are these things?

—*John Keel* (Operation Trojan Horse, *1970)*

When it comes to haunting evidence, nothing has been around as long as ghost photography. Besides capturing the real thing, photography was also used early on by the debunkers of fraudulent spirit and psychic activity—and for every real ghost photo, there are thousands of fakes. During the heyday of the Spiritualist movement, frauds would claim to have the ability to channel the dead and would then take photos of the "spirits" and/or the ectoplasm that would issue forth from the "medium." The methods for performing this trickery involved using double exposures and practical special effects.

Famed illusionist Harry Houdini took great pleasure from exposing such frauds, and early ghost hunters would often find themselves defending their vocation because of such wrongdoings. There were, however, photographs that were taken that still cause much debate today concerning their authenticity. Some are even considered the best examples of spirit photography ever.

Early photos date back as far as the 1860s and even include a snapshot taken by famed Civil War–photographer Matthew Brady of what appears to be a ghost standing in Ford's Theatre, the site of the Abraham Lincoln assassination. Unfortunately, these authentic photos taken by reputable photographers would be outshined by unscrupulous individuals and groups like the infamous Crewe Circle who were proven to be frauds by early ghost hunter Harry Price.

Many of the techniques that early photographers used for photographing the dead are essentially the same today, even though the technology of cameras has come a long way. Before we take a look at the various approaches to spirit photography, let's examine the various types of cameras used for this purpose.

Types of Cameras

There was a time when paranormal investigators steered clear of digital cameras. They believed the format was entirely too easy to manipulate using computer programs and the lack of a negative made authenticating such photos difficult. Since then, it has become apparent that ALL photos can be manipulated using programs like Adobe Photoshop, so the digital camera is now the weapon of choice. Unfortunately, the wide availability of digital cameras (and their ease of use) has caused ghost hunters to overlook other formats of photography that deserve a closer look and a little more use in the field.

The earliest cameras used for photography were film-based cameras, though the film in those days came on single plates rather than rolls of film. Since film costs money, most investigators have stopped using their 35mm cameras. This is a shame. Nothing beats the thrill of getting back a set of developed photographs and finding something paranormal. Of course, that's the very problem that's ushered in the downfall of 35mm cameras: the wait involved with developing film. This also costs money. So it's understandable that you would want to take the bulk of your photographs using a digital camera—but don't give up on film! After all, you can try using infrared film, using different lenses, and other techniques with a 35mm camera.

Another format that's gone by the wayside is the trusty old Polaroid camera. Also known as an Instant or Instamatic camera, there was a time when no photograph was considered as fake-proof as a Polaroid. This is because the photo is developed right before your eyes instead of in a darkroom, so there's no chance of doctoring or changing the photograph before you see it. These cameras are still around, as are the film cartridges, so pick one up if you're interested in checking them out.

Historic Case— The Entity

One of the most intriguing ghost photographs taken in recent years involves the famous "Entity" case of Southern California. In 1974, a young woman named Doris confessed to Dr. Barry Taff and Kerry Gaynor that her home was haunted by a particularly malevolent spirit that would often rape her. When the two investigators visited the home, they found an environment filled with abuse and signs of paranormal activity that included an unusually high barometric pressure and the appearance of multiple apparitions.

A team of investigators, accompanied by author Frank De Felitta, would descend upon the home and witness strange events that culminated with the partial appearance of a male apparition. During the investigation, a series of photographs were taken using a Polaroid instant camera that proved that strange blobs of energy would appear in front of Doris's face when she claimed they were there. The Polaroid would also capture strange arcs of light that would spontaneously appear and shoot across the room.

One of the Polaroid photographs that contained these arcs of light would be authenticated by *Popular Photography* magazine as the genuine article and author De Felitta would write a book about the entire case called *The Entity*. Pick up a copy and read about one of the strangest hauntings ever...

As mentioned previously, by far the most common and preferred camera for the paranormal enthusiast is the digital camera. This style of photography has been honed into a fine art and the availability of software (not to mention traditional photo labs that print photos from your digital camera) is commonplace. There are a few things you may want to consider, though, before deciding on your digital camera purchase:

1. Price. There is a huge spectrum of different brands, features, and accessories. Know in advance how much you want to spend, and then make your purchase based on which camera in your price range fits your needs.

2. Features. Some features are of particular interest to ghost hunters, such as low-light capability, auto and manual focus, battery life, and portability. If you plan to do infra-red or ultraviolet photography, you also will want to make sure the camera can use filters.

3. Resolution. Digital cameras can have a reso-lution as low as 1.5 megapixels and as high as, well … really high. Generally speaking, anything over 5 megapixels is probably going to be fine for ghost hunting. Lower than that, though, and you may have issues when you blow up a photo to a large size or zoom into a specific spot on a photo.

4. Software. One of the perks of digital photog-raphy is the ability to enhance and improve upon your photos using software. Of course, this software can be expensive, so you might want to make sure your camera comes with a free program.

5. Night vision. Night vision in a digital camera? Yes, indeed. Little known to most folks is the fact that Sony makes regular digital cameras that have a "night shot" feature. This is a great thing to have on an investigation.

Dangers of Flash Photography

Since most cameras do not feature any kind of night-vision capability, you will have to decide how you will take photographs in the dark. Most people opt to use the onboard flash for this purpose, but I recommend against this for several reasons.

First, when you use a flash, the sudden bright light will tend to refract and reflect off anything and everything in the area. This includes mirrors, shiny surfaces, dust, water, bugs, you name it. As a result, it is easy to mistake the mundane for something paranormal. This type of photo is single-handedly responsible for the entire mythology surrounding the infamous "orb." Any bit of moisture in the air, on the lens—or airborne dust/pollen—will refract light as a nice, little ball of wispy white matter floating in the air. This is the orb. These are not paranormal objects despite the thousands of folks who photograph them and claim them to be so.

Another drawback to the flash is that it is an extremely strong light. Since any kind of apparition would only be seen because of the light it emanates, a camera's flash will blow out the light of the spirit. Imagine it like this: if you sit a single candle on a table, you will see the glow of the flame on the wall behind it. Now, if you turn on a powerful spotlight and point it at the same wall, you will only see the light from the spotlight. The candle's puny light is obliterated. This is what a flash can do if you try to photograph an apparition with one.

The last point I want to make about avoiding flash photography involves you, the investigator. Sometimes it takes quite a while to get your natural "night eyes" going while you're working in the dark. You're walking along in the pitch black, just able to pick out the pieces of furniture and navigate more easily, and then somebody snaps a photo with a flash and you're blind all over again! Rather than using a flash on your digital or film camera, consider purchasing a small video light that can be attached to your camera. That way you can use a low-light setting, avoid the flash, and still get high-quality photographs.

One way to minimize the impact of your camera's flash is to tape a piece of clear, red gel over it. *That way, the flash is red and of lower intensity. Red lights can actually help out night vision gear as well—and you'll get less reflection off bugs, etc. using a red flash.*

Ghost Story—
The Eldred House

During the shooting of the movie *Ghosts of War*, we visited a historic haunted location in Eldred, Illinois. Tales of apparitions, voices, and objects moving were associated with the location, so we had high hopes of obtaining evidence at the site. To this end, we toured the property, noting the hot spots and individual stories—one of which was the tale of a Native American spirit that had been spotted multiple times along a specific fence row.

Hours into the investigation, the three members of Paranormal Inc. (including myself) would walk up and down the fence, snapping photographs using several different techniques: infrared, 35mm, etc. We would not be disappointed. Brandon, one of our investigators, and I walked side by side taking digital photos, the only difference being that his camera had a slower shutter setting that allowed for more light in his photos.

A review of the photographs would turn up a series of shots that actually shows the spirit of the Native American appearing. At first, there's just a small blur of red light floating in the air adjacent to the fence. Soon, you can make out a part of the actual apparition. The final photo is the full spirit appearing exactly where eyewitnesses said it occurred! It always pays off to pay attention to the information gathered from witnesses—though sometimes a huge grain of salt is also in order.

Shooting in Full Spectrum

As with 35mm cameras, it is possible to shoot in infrared using digital cameras, as well as in the ultraviolet and full spectrum realms. It just takes a few additional steps to do it. There are, basically, three ways to shoot in infrared using a digital camera.

The easiest method to shoot in infrared or ultraviolet is to purchase an IR- or UV-pass filter that fits your digital camera, screw it on, and start taking pictures. Most cameras have this ability, though it will limit you to daytime-only photos. This is because there's only enough available infrared and ultraviolet light during the day to facilitate a clear photo. As with video cameras, you may also need to purchase a neutral-density filter to knock down some of the light for your photos, but this depends on the sensitivity of your digital camera. Just make sure you check your camera's filter size so you purchase the correct size.

Another method for shooting in full spectrum is to simply purchase a digital camera that has a built-in night vision feature. This will allow you to shoot full spectrum at night (though you may need to purchase an infrared or black light to boost the available light). This type of camera will also allow you to shoot in either IR or UV during daylight hours. To do this, place the appropriate filter (IR or UV-pass) on the camera, and then turn on the night vision feature—in this order. Turning a camera's night vision feature on during daylight hours without a filter can damage its sensors.

The third option for full-spectrum photography is the most expensive and involves purchasing an actual full spectrum camera. There are several models of this camera on the

Another inexpensive light to consider purchasing is the common strobe light. *Though it will be practically useless for photography, many swear by strobe lights for helping to see small movements in a room, as well as to catch shadowy apparitions moving about.*

market that are made for forensics work, but they are pricey. Of course, there's a whole sea of companies that also take regular digital cameras and "hack" them to be full spectrum for less money, but you risk getting a low quality product with limited resolution. So, buyer beware!

As I mentioned above, in almost all occasions involved with shooting full spectrum at night, you will need to supply additional lighting. Infrared lights/illuminators are easy to find and are quite affordable. Ultraviolet lights, on the other hand, can be expensive and even dangerous. A lot of UV lights are made for plant growth and for tanning beds; these types of bulbs can hurt your vision and even cause skin problems, so you will want to purchase simple "black lights" if you want to work with UV.

Tips for Using Cameras

In a lot of ways, working with still cameras is similar to working with video recorders. There are a few steps that you can take to insure that your photographs will turn out well.

1. If possible, use a tripod. Though in many instances, you will want to carry your camera around with you, consider using a mobile tripod (or even a monopod) that will allow you to steady your shots. This will be especially helpful if you're working in a low-light situation or are using a long shutter speed.

2. Avoid the flash. This is for the reasons already mentioned.

3. Survey your surroundings. Since you won't want any shiny surfaces around to reflect light or want any excessive shadows in your photos, observe the area you're working in prior to taking photos there.

4. Perform routine maintenance. Since anything on a camera's lens can cause images to be blurry, or to even appear as something paranormal, you should clean your camera regularly.

5. Keep plenty of expendables. Make sure you have enough film, batteries, etc., to get through an investigation. This may mean purchasing additional rechargeable batteries for digital cameras.

6. Be mindful of your resolution. Most digital cameras have multiple settings for photos and it's worth using the highest available format during your investigations. If possible, purchase a camera that can shoot in a

RAW format; this style of photo has fantastic resolution and lends itself to adjustments in photo-editing programs.

7. Do you have enough memory? Digital cameras require memory cards to store photos; since you'll be taking high-quality photos with large file sizes, make sure you purchase a memory card that's large enough to accommodate a few hundred photos. This may mean purchasing extra memory cards.

If you take the necessary steps to control the quality of your photography, you will have a more pleasant experience analyzing/reviewing your photos after an investigation.

Analyzing and Editing Photos

So now you are sitting at your desk or kitchen table and reviewing the photographic evidence you captured during your investigation. If these photos are physical objects—meaning they are printed out on photo paper—you will want to carefully scan each photo for any anomalies. A simple way to do this is to imagine a clock on the photo. Look at the top central area of the photo, where twelve o'clock would be, then work your way slowly around the edge of the photo in a clockwise manner. When you get back to where you started, move closer to the center of the photo and repeat again. Do this until you've covered every part of the photograph.

If you are working with digital photos, your review will need a few more things: a computer, something to take notes on (can also be your computer), and a photo-editing program. Since you will most likely already have a computer or you wouldn't have purchased a digital camera, let's talk about photo-editing programs.

The most well-known program of this sort would have to be Adobe Photoshop. It is an industry standard and it sets the bar for features and functionality. Unfortunately, it can also be quite difficult to learn if you don't have much experience with these types of programs. Of course, there is a basic version of this program called Adobe Photoshop Elements, too. Other choices for photo editing are out there, but they are mostly variations of Photoshop, so compare features of these programs before purchasing.

There are also a couple of free alternatives to photo editing as well. Paranormal equipment guru Bill Chappell offers a free photo-editing program on his website (www .digitaldowsing.com) called Image PX and the free GIMP photo editor is a popular choice for those involved with the paranormal (www.gimp.org). Another option for a free program is to purchase a digital camera that comes with free software. This is more common than you might think, and many of these programs are rich with features.

Once you have your program, and you have uploaded your digital photos to your computer, you will want to open the program and check out each photo. Use the same method of clockwise observation mentioned above, and when necessary, use the "Zoom" tool in your program to take a closer look at anything that seems out of place (to include light and shadows). Since photo editors have a lot of tools for improving upon and enhancing your photos, you can also take advantage of a few of these features.

It is generally unacceptable among paranormal investigators to alter photos in any way that might make the mundane appear to be evidence of a haunting—but some tools can be used without fear of accusation of wrongdoing. These features generally include the auto-adjustments you can apply to a photo that affects how light/dark the photo is, the contrast, and the color. Zooming in to one spot of a photo and exporting that section is also fine, as is cropping a photo to keep only what you need. Just be careful not to cut out anything of significance and remember to keep a copy of the original photo as well.

Once you have altered any photo, you will have to save that photo as a new file before moving on to the next shot. To do this, go under the "File" tab at the top of the program and select "Save As" to save your new, improved photo on your computer. You may also want to save your photos in a file format that's generally easy to use on different websites, such as JPEG.

So, how do you recognize a paranormal photo? Well, if there's a full apparition of a person smiling at the camera, you can be pretty sure that is paranormal! Other than that, it may take some careful study to determine an authentic ghost photo. If the object is not shaped like a human, chances are it will be an object that's ball-shaped, a streak of light, or an area of smoke/mist.

If you have a streak of light in the photo, the first thing you want to pay attention to is the other objects in frame. If they are blurry, chances are the light streak is a product of the camera moving when you snapped the photo. If everything is in focus, then the light itself was moving. Firefly? Flashlight in the distance? Zoom in and examine it closely;

exhaust all attempts to debunk the photo before proclaiming it to be paranormal.

Balls of light are also commonly photographed in the field. If you were using a flash, pay close attention to the object. Does it appear to have wings and/or legs? Probably a bug then. Analyze the photo closely; most semi-transparent, round objects pan out to be dust or moisture in the air or on the lens. If you weren't using a flash, then the light is probably self-illuminating. This is a good thing. If you can rule out any man-made, roaming lights in the area you took the photo, then there's the possibility of this being a "ghost light," a naturally occurring paranormal phenomena.

Another commonly taken photo in the field is that of a strange mist or smoke. Most often, though, these fall in the same category as the infamous "orb"...

Orbs and Mists

Of all the paranormal "debates" that span this field, none are more polarizing than the disposition of orbs. Traditionally, orbs were glowing balls of light that would be seen with the naked eye while performing an investigation. On occasion, these orbs would even be captured in a photograph or video clip. Unfortunately, for every genuine orb captured by these devices, there are about 100,000 false orbs. These would generally be particles of dust in the air, drops of moisture, or bugs.

Since so many of these false orbs began appearing in photos, the real ones are now known as either ghost lights, will-'o-the-wisps, or even sprite lights. And the word "orbs" has become a moniker associated with non-paranormal activity. It's really that simple and it requires no debate. If you see a strange light that's unexplainable, that's a ghost light. If you get a photo with a bunch of circular, semi-transparent objects drifting through the air (dust), you have captured orbs that can be disregarded.

Right there with the orbs, though, is the subject of mists. Since most ghost hunting takes place at night, there are a lot of different natural things going on that can mislead paranormal investigators into believing they are shooting a spirit in the form of a "mist." Such things include changes of temperature that can cause plants to "steam," moisture in the air, and even smoke that results from hot breath in a cold environment. It is not difficult to take pictures during a cold night and to accidentally capture your own breath in a photograph. This is, of course, not paranormal and should be disregarded.

Other problems with photos include shots being out of focus, a dirty lens, refraction of light, and matrixing. As mentioned in the video chapter, matrixing is the human eye seeing something that's random and making it into something paranormal. (Our brains often attempt to find patterns in chaos.) Most often, this occurs whenever light bounces off a surface, making the natural imperfections/dirt appear to be part of an apparition. This is the reason you will want to avoid using flash photography and shooting at reflective surfaces (window, mirrors, etc.).

Working with photography is a pretty straightforward affair: you shoot the photos, review them for paranormal activity, improve upon them if necessary, and archive them. As you perform more and more investigations—and you become familiar with your particular camera—your photographs will get consistently better. So never fear if you make a few mistakes the first time out with a new camera. This is all part of the learning process.

Now that we've gone over audio, video, and photographic evidence, it's time we moved on into a realm that's less familiar to those new to ghost hunting: environmental monitoring.

six

Environmental Monitoring

There are many ways of opening the doors of perception.
Not all of them enable you to control what comes through
the open doors, or to get them shut again.

—*Guy Lyon Playfair* (The Indefinite Boundary, *1976)*

When we are performing a paranormal investigation, we are essentially looking for changes in the environment that cannot be explained by conventional means. Audio recorders, camcorders, and cameras can capture a lot of the more obvious changes: apparitions appearing, disembodied voices speaking from thin air, and even objects moving by themselves. But this is really just scratching the surface. There are a lot of factors that can change within a location that can't be monitored using these mainstream devices.

With the popularity of ghost hunting and paranormal television at an all-time high, new devices are being built almost daily for investigators. Most of these are spinoffs of scientific gear that have been modified to specifically help ghost hunters—and some devices are unique to the field entirely. One of the great things about this new popularity is that a lot of the scientific equipment has now dropped in price significantly, making it affordable for most new groups.

Before I explain some of the more obscure, new approaches to environmental monitoring, let's take a look at some of the more traditional, time-tested equipment.

EMF Detectors

Since the days of the Spiritualists, the subject of electromagnetic energy has been of interest to paranormal investigators. The American Psychic Institute developed a device they dubbed a "uluometer" in the 1920s that would make a loud whine whenever electromagnetic energy came near it. They would use this to help track strange electromagnetic fields in a haunted location. Today, we still believe spirits most likely emit an electromagnetic field and we have a similar device for tracking them that's known as an EMF detector.

It is important to note that EMFs (electromagnetic fields) are relevant today for more reasons than just hauntings. Exposure to high levels of EMFs can cause adverse effects to a person's health, including nausea, headaches, and (possibly) cancer. Because of this, manufacturers began cranking out EMF detectors to help people monitor the levels of electromagnetic radiation coming from power lines, electrical wiring, and even cell phones. Oftentimes, if a home has high levels of EMFs (usually 100+ milligauss), this can cause a person to feel paranoid, nauseated, and even hallucinate.

If you do a quick Internet search for EMF detectors, you are going to find yourself suddenly face to face with about a hundred different choices! This has to do with the various levels of quality, types of detectors, and even what the individual devices were created specifically to do. General choices include getting an analog or digital detector and if the detector is a single-axis device or a tri-axis style meter.

Analog and digital EMF detectors basically measure electromagnetic energy the same way. The only difference is in the display and how you read the device. An analog EMF detector will feature a little needle and graph that looks like a speedometer—if there are no EMFs present, the needle will be on "0." As you encounter electromagnetic fields, the needle will start to go up. Analog EMF detectors (as well as digital) measure EMF's in milligauss, (mG) a unit of measurement created by Johann Carl Friedrich Gauss to monitor magnetic strength.

A digital EMF detector acts just like an analog detector, but the readout will be with digital numbers—much like the numbers on a calculator. Both versions of the EMF detector can work for you equally well, though you should pay attention to the *type* of EMF detector you purchase. The most common type of detector (and the most inexpensive) is the single-axis EMF detector.

The term "single axis" simply means there's only one sensor in the device—and this sensor can be inaccurately high with its reading. Since nobody knows just how high a reading should be to indicate a ghostly presence, this device will work just fine for your investigation if you're using it to simply find and track the odd electromagnetic field. Popular examples of this type of EMF detector include the cell sensor–style device and the widely used K2 or K-II–style meter. If you are looking for accurate scientific measurements of an electromagnetic field, though, you will have to step up to the more expensive tri-axis style meter.

The tri-axis meter, unlike the single axis, has three onboard sensors in the meter that help the device to obtain consistent and accurate readings no matter what angle or direction you point the device. There are several manufacturers of this type of meter and these usually have additional features that make the extra expense worth it. These extras can include audible alarms that go off when EMFs are present, additional types of detection (static electricity, etc.), and even backlit readouts that help you read the device in complete darkness.

I have found over the years that both detectors can come in handy, so it's worth your time and money to purchase at least one of each. It's also nice if one of your EMF detectors has an audible alarm; some cell sensor–type detectors will beep and light up when you encounter an electromagnetic field and there are several tri-axis detectors that do this as well. These are great to place in a room to warn you when there is a change in EMFs there.

If you plan to purchase an EMF detector to carry around with you, almost every type will work for this, though you might want to avoid any detector that picks up natural electromagnetic fields. Our human bodies actually put out weak EMFs (one of the reasons we believe ghosts do as well) and a natural detector will pick this up, so you may not want it around yourself and other investigators. These are best left to monitor an area since they can pick up extremely weak electromagnetic fields.

Also, if you plan to carry around an EMF detector, you will want to use the device properly. Hold the meter nice and steady in your hand while moving it slowly and deliberately around you to detect any fields. Keep in mind that bad wiring, electronic devices, and your cell phone (even when it's not receiving a phone call) can give off readings on an EMF detector, so be sure any encounters you have are truly paranormal before getting too excited. It's also a great strategy to place an EMF detector in a paranormal hot spot and then to point a camcorder at it to record any changes.

If a haunted location consistently picks up strange EMFs, you may consider purchasing a frequency counter as well. Since there is a whole spectrum of EMFs, a frequency counter will tell you the exact frequency the electromagnetic field is broadcasting at vs. the strength of the field (what the EMF detector tells you). Correlating paranormal activity to a specific range of frequencies would be a great step toward proving the existence of ghosts.

One final thing worth noting about EMF detectors is that there are certain types of meters that can also go into the realm of ELFs (extremely low frequencies) and even detect less than 1 milligauss fields. These can be useful in locations that have no power at all. Normally, though, even good electrical wiring can affect these types of detectors, so they will not work well for you in most situations.

Though certain devices are known for giving off strong electromagnetic fields (microwave ovens, television sets, alarm clocks, etc.) that can fool you into thinking you've gotten some paranormal activity, these can also work in your favor.

The Paranormal Battery

Not only do paranormal investigators believe that ghosts are made up of electromagnetic fields, but most believe that spirits require energy to perform any actions. Normally, this energy would be obtained naturally from electronic devices, the environment, and people (remember, we have EMFs, too) in the area. It's because of this that batteries are called "ghost bait" in the field and, all too often, our gear is sucked dry while performing an investigation.

> ### Ghost Story—
> ### Private Case in Missouri
> While investigating a haunted, historic home in Cape Girardeau, Missouri, every member of my paranormal group would experience an ongoing drainage of all our batteries. This was particularly frustrating because the home had no power, so we were dependent upon batteries for the investigation. In the space of one single hour, two audio recorders, a camcorder, and an EMF detector were all sucked dry!
>
> Realizing that this was not ordinary behavior for these devices (and remembering stocking them earlier the same evening with fresh batteries), it became clear that there was most likely a spirit of some sort attempting to draw energy. Of course, we wanted the spirit to have the necessary energy needed to make itself known to us—just not at the expense of our gear! So we placed an electromagnetic field generator in the room that seemed to be experiencing the most battery drainage.

Immediately, things started happening. Our camcorder caught a strange, spectral smear of light moving through the room, our audio recorders began getting quality EVPs, and one investigator was even touched by the entity. If you're investigating a location and you notice a lot of batteries going dead, you may want to pay attention to this ...

But what if we could supply a sort of "energy source" for ghosts to draw power from? Theoretically, this would allow entities to do more of the things we like to see and hear during investigations. In addition to the aforementioned household items, there are a few devices you can construct or purchase that can help you supply this energy. The first of these was actually created by inventor Nikola Tesla and is known as the Tesla Coil.

The Tesla Coil is a transformer circuit that produces a high voltage current of AC electricity. Since these can be quite dangerous (as in electrocution), care should be taken in constructing and using these devices. In all actuality, it's probably better to avoid using a Tesla Coil and to purchase or make the safer alternative: the Van de Graaf generator.

Constructed in 1929 by American physicist Robert J. Van de Graaf, this machine is a metal ball (usually on a stand) that emits a static electricity field. They generally produce a field that is harmless to humans, but some can crank out high levels of electricity and should be avoided for safety reasons. You know those glass plasma balls that have colored electric bolts in them that shoot out when you touch them? These are a rudimentary (and safe) version of the Van de Graaf generator and can be used by you in the

Want a low-tech solution to the EMF detector?

Try a traditional compass. If you walk around an area with a compass and suddenly see the needle move from the proper direction to point the wrong way, this will be an electromagnetic field that's attracting the compass and, possibly, a ghost.

field. They are usually called plasma balls and can be purchased through numerous online vendors.

Another way to produce safe energy for spirits to utilize is to construct or purchase an EM pump/generator that emits a low level of EMFs into the environment. An online search will bring you a couple different manufacturers of this type of device, as well as plans to build your own. Just keep in mind that once you use any of these generators in an area, your EMF detectors will become essentially useless.

You will also want to discontinue the use of any generated EMFs if anyone suddenly feels ill or exhibits any of the symptoms I mentioned above that are associated with a hypersensitivity to electromagnetic fields. Know that "bad feeling" in the pit of your stomach? It's not always your instincts kicking in!

Weather and Temperature Monitors

When you talk to inhabitants of haunted places, they will often tell you about encountering "cold spots."

These are thought to indicate the presence of a spirit. The reason for this is that we are surrounded by thermal energy (heat) in the air—energy that spirits can use to perform work that manifests as paranormal activity. In other words, as a spirit draws thermal energy from the environment, that area cools down. Because of this, the use of weather stations and digital thermometers has become commonplace.

In addition to measuring the temperature, most weather stations also can give you additional weather statistics, such as the relative humidity. If you are going to purchase a station, I suggest picking up a unit that measures barometric pressure. Researchers over the years have discovered that in cases where poltergeist activity is present, there are often drastic changes in barometric pressure just prior to an event (such as in the Entity case mentioned earlier). This could be useful with helping you predict activity.

Of course, weather stations are made to stay in one location—though you can purchase some models that have a monitoring unit and several remote sensors. This can be especially great for the investigator since you can place the monitoring station at your rally point and post remote sensors in rooms with paranormal activity. Then, whoever is manning the live-monitoring station can keep track of any drastic temperature or barometric changes throughout the site.

If you don't mind spending a little extra money, you can even purchase devices that connect directly to a computer to monitor and record environmental data. Some of these monitor the weather only, but more and more companies (including those that specialize in paranormal gear) are adding on the capability to monitor changes in static electricity

146 · *Chapter Six*

and electromagnetic fields as well. This can be a great asset to your investigation.

In addition to stationary thermometers/weather stations, you may also consider picking up a portable digital thermometer that can be carried by an investigator. These can take an instant measurement of the ambient temperature around you so you can quickly identify the appearance of (or lack of) a cold spot. There are a few different styles of digital thermometers on the market, so you will want to make sure of a few things before making a purchase:

1. Does it measure ambient temperature? A lot of the pistol-type digital thermometers measure temperature by emitting a laser. The temperature you are reading is the spot that the laser is hitting. These devices are fine as long as they also have the option to measure the air immediately around the unit (usually referred to as ambient temperature). Sometimes they will have an external probe to this effect that looks like a mini-antenna that sticks out from the unit.

2. How accurate is the thermometer? There are a lot of different brands of digital thermometers out there with varying degrees of accuracy, so be sure to check into the "variance" or accuracy. A 1 to 3 degree variance is acceptable. More than that and your readings are not accurate enough to be of scientific use.

3. What unit of measurement does the device use? Sounds obvious, but it isn't. If you use Celsius or Fahrenheit exclusively, make sure your thermometer can read that unit of measurement.

4. Price. Shop around. Again, there are lots of models and brands, and some are extremely expensive. If you're only interested in measuring ambient temperature and could not care less about any laser capabilities, you can pick up a digital thermometer quite cheaply.

Though you often see ghost hunters on television constantly walking around with their digital thermometer in their hand like a gunslinger, this is a device that's best used in moderation. Ideally, you would have the thermometer on your person so that when you encounter a cold spot, you can take out the thermometer and take a quick reading. If you believe there's a cold spot present, before leaving the area, examine the surroundings. Did an air conditioner kick on? Is there a draft coming in? Do your best to debunk a cold spot before conceding it to be paranormal.

Ghost Story— The Talbott Tavern

Tales concerning the ghosts at the old Talbott Tavern in Bardstown, Kentucky, are all over the Internet—and the owners/operators of the bed and breakfast can tell you even more. When I visited this location, I was told a few of its more interesting stories, including one that placed famed gunfighter Jesse James as the first person to see a ghost at the tavern. According to the tale, James was relaxing in his room when he suddenly noticed a strange man was standing at the foot of his bed. Fearing the intruder was a lawman, he drew his revolver and promptly fired. To his amazement, the man did not react at all to the shots. He simply disappeared right before his eyes. Today, this room is named for the noted outlaw, and the bullet holes from this affair can still be seen in the wall!

As my investigation of the property progressed, I became more interested in a different story; according to locals, a young woman had committed suicide in the ballroom of the tavern by hanging herself from a chandelier. Since then, her apparition has been seen in this room and paranormal activity is quite common. A local ghost tour in Bardstown makes this ballroom a regular stop during their trek, so this tale is quite well known in the area.

While I was working in the ballroom, I noticed some strange activity—first on my EMF detector, then on my digital thermometer. I was sitting in a chair doing some EVP work when I felt a massive blast of cold air hit me. I took a quick reading and confirmed it was a 12-degree drop in temperature! Moments later, a door suddenly opened by itself; the handle actually jiggled, then the door swung open in a slow, deliberate manner. Activity then ramped up to the point that I could ask the spirit to approach me and touch my hand that was holding the EMF detector. The detector would slowly start to beep and light up, and then get faster—and soon I would feel the pressure of a spectral hand drop on mine.

I would record much of this on audio and video recorders, but on the scientific end of things, it was nice to also get environmental data during the investigation. My EMF detectors would pick up 18 to 21 milligauss jumps in electromagnetic energy and the digital thermometer would record the aforementioned drops in temperature. Backing up your personal experiences with scientific data is always a good thing during an investigation.

Motion Detectors

Since it's practically impossible to be in every room of a location at once, paranormal investigators rely on a lot of different gear to help monitor different places. In a huge way, this is a primary function of audio and video recorders. Another way we often stakeout an area is to place a motion detector there.

Motion detectors come in all shapes, sizes, and styles, so it's important to note that the type of detector we use in the field is usually of the passive-infrared (PIR) variety. These types of detectors project an infrared field that, when broken, causes the device to emit an alarm. It's thought that, since these detectors are scanning in infrared, that they are particularly useful for detecting the presence of a light/shadow anomaly—the two ways that entities are often seen during an investigation.

Shopping for a PIR motion detector is relatively easy and you will find three general styles to choose from. The first is the lower-end projection-type detector. These small devices (usually about the size of a pack of cigarettes) are placed in a room and shoot a cone of detection out into an area. If anything breaks that cone, the alarm goes off.

The second style of detector works exactly the same way, but is usually accompanied by more data or even a camera. These are usually "game cameras" that hunters use to track their prey. With this style of detector, when something breaks the cone of detection, a small video clip or series of photographs is taken—often in infrared. Good game cameras even tag the video/photos with the current time, date, and temperature. This can be extremely useful in the field—especially during outside investigations, since these cameras are made to be placed in the woods.

The last category of detector involves a transmitter and a receiver. Instead of simply shooting a field into a room, these detectors also receive the other end of the field, creating a beam that will activate an alarm when broken. This type of detector is especially useful for monitoring an object that's known for moving or a door that's said to open by itself, etc. Since the beam is quite controlled and confined, this kind of detector will also allow for investigators to walk all around it without sounding the alarm.

One of the more interesting techniques that has sprung up in the last year or so is the use of "laser grids" to monitor movement in an area. These grids can be as simple as a laser pointer that's had a kaleidoscope attachment or scope placed on the end of it (these are available online for a reasonable price) or as complicated as a portable laser light show that projects patterns/designs.

To use a laser grid correctly, you will want to choose a static pattern; after all, you are ghost hunting, not setting up an impromptu disco! This pattern should be projected into an area of a room known for objects moving or shadowy apparitions. The use of the laser pattern will (generally) allow you to see movement more easily. Pair up this technique with a video camera, and it's a great way to monitor an area for activity.

If you decide to try this technique in the field, you should be extremely wary of the laser itself. Many of these devices are extremely powerful, so contact between the laser's beam and your skin and eyes should be avoided. Once you set it up, investigators should do their best to not step in front of the laser at any time. Seriously, you can really mess up your eyes if you aren't careful, so use every precaution you can to keep your team out of harm's way.

Another recent, popular device that's being used for motion detection is the "geophone." This piece of gear is designed to pick up vibrations and to let you know about them through a variety of methods. They were created for detecting seismic activity, but paranormal engineers have now tweaked these devices to pick up vibrations as small as a person clapping their hands. When a geophone picks up movement/vibrations, it usually lights up in some way to warn you. I don't have to tell you that, while the use of a geophone sounds like a great idea, there are a large number of problems with them in the field...

There's going to be almost no area that is completely free of vibrations. Everything from your team walking around to passing traffic to an air conditioner kicking on will set these things off. Furthermore, since they pick up ALL vibrations—not just the paranormal ones—you will NEVER know if the vibrations are an indication of ghostly activity. To make matters even worse, these devices can be hard to purchase and quite expensive. When you've been ghost hunting for a very long time, and you're itching to try out a new gadget, consider getting a geophone. But for motion detecting that's of a more practical use, go with the other methods mentioned.

Ion Counters and Projectors

Associating ions with the presence of a ghost is one of the most interesting realms of the paranormal. If you were to ask a room full of ghost hunters about using an ion detector during an investigation, most would tell you that you should do so. However, if you asked them why you should use an ion counter/detector, you'd be lucky to even get an answer!

Ions are associated with hauntings in two ways: they are part of an electrical discharge, and they can affect emotion. The first reason has everything to do with the idea that souls/ghosts are most likely made up of electrical or electromagnetic energy and the second has a lot to do with the psychological atmosphere of a location and the idea that emotions can attract spirits. Let's take a closer look at the first reason.

Whenever there is an electric discharge of any kind, ions are formed. These tend to attach themselves to molecules in the area and can create an excess of either negative or positive ions that can make the air feel charged. Because of this, any excessive amount of ions could be an indication that something of an electrical nature has occurred in the area—such as ghostly activity for instance. Ion detectors/counters are a great way to track these areas of electrical disturbance.

On the other end of the stick, scientists also have proven that when the air is full of ions, it can actually affect the way humans feel and behave. Negative ions can help create an environment charged with positive emotions and are associated with sunny days, beaches, etc. Positive ions tend to cause depression and usually occur when a place is shut off from the outside—like in the wintertime. Since this is the case, many people believe a scary feeling or a sense of dread in a place may simply be an overabundance of positive ions affecting the people.

Some investigators have gone so far as to claim that specific ions can attract certain types of spirits; positive ions are thought to attract the demonic/bad spirits and negative ions are thought to attract good/once-living spirits. Conversely, the introduction of certain ions to the environment are associated with also repelling ghosts (i.e., project negative ions into the air to drive away bad spirits). All of these theories are quite interesting and can be tested to an extent by purchasing an ion counter/detector and, optionally, an ion projector.

An ion projector is a device that you can purchase from health stores to fill a room with negative ions. As mentioned above, negative ions are associated with good mental health, and this is a good way to make everyone feel better during

An inexpensive way to introduce negative ions to an area is to burn a 'Himalayan Rock Salt Lamp.' *These are lamps made of huge chunks of rock salt, with a bulb inside the salt. These lamps emit negative ions when they are used, and they can be easily purchased online for a low price.*

months of little sunshine. Of course, there's nothing stopping you from using a negative ion projector for testing the "attraction" theory as well.

Geiger Counters

This is another rarely used piece of gear. A Geiger counter picks up levels of radioactive activity in the air and functions in many ways like an ion detector. The idea that ghosts emit radiation is not very popular in the world of the paranormal—and there has been little evidence over the years to suggest that this could be the case. At one time, Geiger counters were a common item (especially during the Cold War when the fear of a nuclear assault was prevalent), so it would make sense that folks would at some point try them out on an investigation. Of course, there are a lot of reasons to shoot down the radiation theory…

First of all, if ghosts emitted radiation, they would be harmful to the living. Since some places have been haunted for centuries, it doesn't make sense that nobody has ever reported becoming sick. If the levels of radiation in a location are extremely low, they may not be strong enough to make anyone sick, but they should still turn up as a reading on a Geiger counter. To my knowledge, nobody has ever correlated radioactive activity with a haunting. The Geiger counter is, most definitely, a piece of gear you can skip!

A typical assortment of gear. Photo by Rich Newman.

Static Electricity and Dowsing Rods

Ambient static electricity in the air is so similar to charged ions that in most cases it is not necessary to have a static electricity detector *and* an ion counter. It does make sense that static electricity should be present when a spirit is around—and even that a ghost may actually tap into static electricity in the air for power (such as during an electrical thunderstorm), so maybe it is worth your time to look for one of these devices.

Some EMF detectors (usually the tri-field meter models) can actually measure static electricity in the air in addition to electromagnetic fields, though these types of units cost a bit more. You can also opt to go a low-tech route: dowsing rods.

Dating back to the Renaissance, the practice of using divining rods is still common throughout the paranormal world. Users of these rods claim that spirits can interact with them by crossing or uncrossing the rods to answer yes/ no questions. Most modern dowsing rods are made of metals that conduct electricity, though some insist upon using traditional wooden rods or a single Y-shaped stick.

While it is true that some metals conduct electricity and could service as a conduit for ghostly electric currents, there are serious problems involved with the use of dowsing rods. Primarily, the rods are held within a person's hands and can typically swing quite freely. All it takes is a slight dip of one hand to make a rod swing around to cross the other. Because of this, it's hard to tell if you are getting an "answer" from a spirit or simply dropping a hand slightly (an action that's easy to do in a dark room without even knowing it).

Paranormal-Specific Gear

With the newfound popularity of ghost hunting on the rise, it only makes sense that manufacturers of electronic detection devices would get in on the craze. There are quite a few companies (and individuals) that now make equipment designed especially for ghost hunters. These are often great things, since sometimes it's hard to find gear that specifically fits our needs. (Really, who else needs an ultraviolet light illuminator?)

A quick search on the Internet will take you to a lot of these companies, but you will want to make sure to separate what's being sold for genuine research from things that are made for entertainment purposes. Examples of genuine gear will be IR/UV illuminators, devices made to track changes in environmental conditions, and improvements upon existing audio/photographic/video equipment.

But whether you purchase gear from the general market, or you are getting it built by paranormal tech gurus, you need to spend a lot of quality time learning how to use your gear. I cannot even begin to count the times I went on an investigation with another paranormal group that brought gear they had never used. Or if they had used it, they didn't fully understand how to use it correctly. This goes for cameras, camcorders, EMF detectors, etc. Equipment is useless if you don't have the knowledge to implement it into an investigation correctly!

It's also a great idea to document the various ways you deploy your gear. Some pieces of equipment seem to work better when they are stationary or are used alone without other gear present (some things can interfere with each other—especially wireless devices) and some devices are made for being mobile. There are also investigators who like to saturate a location with as much surveillance gear as possible, while others on a lower budget are more strategic with their placement.

There are different approaches to exploring and investigating the unknown, and none are necessarily any better than the others. But some things work better for some people. So experiment! Now that you have all of your gear together, it's time for us to put it all together during the course of your investigation and to discuss the actual chain of investigation. In Paranormal Inc., we use a simple but straightforward method for ghost hunting that we call DICE.

seven

DICE

If you want to upset the law that all crows are black, you mustn't seek to show that no crows are; it is enough if you prove one single crow to be white.

—William James (The Indefinite Boundary, *Guy Lyon Playfair, 1976*)

Since I first started investigating the paranormal many years ago, technology and the availability of information has soared through the roof. Today, ghost hunters have more tools at their disposal than ever before—this includes books, television programs, and gadgets galore. But most of this means zilch when you are actually standing in your first haunted place and are suddenly faced with, "What's next?"

After numerous cases of trial and error, I learned long ago that some things work and many things do not. Once you've done a few paranormal investigations, you will also start to notice patterns: some things seem to precede others, some actions often escalate activity, and so on. So I started to formulate a system for tackling investigations—one that would allow for events to happen "outside the lines," meaning paranormal activity didn't HAVE to happen just one way.

Author attempting to interact with an entity.
Courtesy of Paranormal Inc.

What we figured out pretty quickly was the *interactivity* of ghost hunting. There seems to be a sort of symbiotic relationship between spirits and those who investigate them—a relationship that can quickly cause events to escalate when done correctly. This pattern of discovery, interaction, and documentation soon earned a name: DICE.

DICE stands for Detect, Interact, Capture, and Escalate, and it is the foundation of every investigation I perform. And the best part of this approach is that it provides a step-by-step method for investigating a haunting that even a novice investigator can master. It also takes everything we've learned about ghost hunting so far and puts it all together for a successful ghost hunt. So, that said, let's take a look at the first step of DICE: Detect.

DICE—Detect

Before you can ever get that first piece of great evidence of a haunting, you will first have to find a ghost! It's a well-known fact in the paranormal field that spirits don't show up on cue. Even the most haunted of spots can suddenly go flat when everyone wants to see a ghost. So how do you track down your elusive quarry? It's best to start simply...

During your initial walkthrough, several hot spots (places where activity is common) should have been pointed out. You will want to station investigators in these places to perform a vigil. As I mentioned in chapter two, a vigil basically means sitting still and paying attention to what's going on around you. Maintain silence and listen for all the little things that happen in a location—natural and paranormal. With any luck, you will notice something of a ghostly nature. Maybe a sound, maybe a sight. At the very least, you will notice a lot of things that aren't paranormal (things like the house settling, ice makers, air conditioners), and knowing these mundane sounds will help you later on when you're listening to your audio and watching your video.

If after performing a vigil you still have not detected anything, it will be time to turn to your environmental-monitoring gear. Your audio and video gear will already be stationed in various locations to capture footage, but this will be of no use to you during your actual investigation. Anything captured with this equipment will turn up in the review, long after you have gone. It will be your EMF detectors, infrared thermometers and other environmental gear that will help you detect any ghosts while you are there.

Once again, begin with the highest probability areas. Slowly make your way around each nook and cranny of an area, and then do room-to-room search. You are looking for any anomalies that contradict the base readings you took during your walkthrough. Anything of significant difference should be investigated and possibly debunked. If the location is, indeed, haunted, a thorough search should turn up something.

Of course, once you've tapped the hot spots, you should go on to the other areas within the location. There is a theory among ghost hunters that spirits will attempt to avoid the living on occasion (hey, everybody wants privacy once in a while), so if you find yourself in a place that has ghost stories about every room but one ... well, this just may be the place a spirit goes for "time out."

Because actually finding a spirit often can be the most difficult step to an investigation, many paranormal groups turn to psychics for assistance. I have found this to be a detriment to the field of parapsychology. There can be many reasons for not detecting a ghost—the most obvious being that the place may simply not be haunted! Over the years, I've noticed that a lot of ghost hunters encounter difficulties because they do not know how to use their gear properly, they resort to provocation too soon, or they lack the patience needed to find something that is truly paranormal.

Because of this, they turn to psychics. They believe the "psychic" is providing instant information, they get a cheap thrill out of having a ghost pointed out for them, and they don't have to put in a lot of time or effort. Do not fall into this trap! Besides the fact that you'll get no tangible evidence from using a psychic, the false information they usually put out will have you investigating the wrong areas, asking the wrong questions, and otherwise going astray.

Working under the assumption that the place you are investigating is actually haunted, once you've performed a vigil and done a thorough room-to-room sweep for paranormal activity, you should have found something—if you've performed your investigation correctly. And it's perfectly fine if this "something" is quite subtle. Once you identify this anomaly, it's important to follow up immediately. Your goal now is to interact with any spirit present.

DICE—Interact

Okay, so you've detected the possible presence of a ghost. In order to capture anything on the multitude of devices at your disposal (the third element of DICE), you will first have to get the spirits to play along with you and to reveal themselves. The easiest—and first—way you should attempt to do this is to simply act like the ghost is a living person.

Since you cannot know for sure who the entity is, it's best to do this with a first person, present tense, gender-neutral approach. To elaborate, think of this technique as a conversation with a person you cannot see or hear. If the particular haunting you are investigating is of a "residual" nature, this approach will have no effect. However, if you are dealing with an intelligent spirit, this style will ensure that you do not anger or upset him or her by making assumptions concerning gender, identity, etc. You also are acknowledging that the ghost is still alive in a sense and this, in itself, can encourage interaction.

I also recommend beginning this type of interaction in a friendly manner. If after an extended amount of time nothing is happening to confirm there is a presence with you at the location, you can then move on to a more aggressive style. It should be noted, though, that not all spirits react positively to provocation. In many cases, the use of derogatory language can drive a ghost into hiding, or simply make them ignore you. If a spirit is "intelligent," it seems only reasonable that a negative approach could cause a negative reaction.

That said, in most cases, it will take more than just conversation to get good interaction with a spirit. A good second move would be to perform a participatory technique that will allow an entity to indicate his/her presence. Examples of this include "table tipping," deploying a pendulum, or using a "trigger object." Let's take a look at these three approaches.

Using Participation

During the heyday of Spiritualism, holding a séance in one's home was the craze. It was not unusual to find a local medium, invite some friends over, and spend the evening attempting to talk to the dead. As mentioned earlier in this book, the vast majority of these mediums were actually charlatans who made their living off duping gullible loved ones into believing they were talking to dead relatives. But as it's often pointed out, some good things can manage to come out of bad situations!

Despite the fact that most Spiritualists were never actually talking to any spirits, they did manage to come up with a few good methods for doing so. The first of these techniques is called table tipping.

The easiest way to explain table tipping is to think of it as a séance without the medium. Basically, you find a lightweight table (those little, fold-up card tables are perfect), have at least two people sit at the table with their palms or fingertips lightly on the surface, and then proceed to carry on a conversation with any spirits who may be present. The theory behind this approach is that the bio-energy/EMFs emitted from the human beings gathered around the table can be used by a ghost to make the table move, bang, or jump.

Since you should always be coupling the things you do in an investigation with scientific/electronic gear, the best approach to performing a controlled table tipping session is this:

1. Go with the fingertip approach. If only fingertips are lightly resting against the table's surface, it will be difficult for any one person to manipulate the table and fake a response.

2. Since actually moving an object—especially as large as a table—can be a difficult task for a spirit, begin by asking for simple knock responses. It can be a "one knock for yes, two knocks for no" approach or simply ask for a knock when you state anything that is correct.

3. Station a video camera and an audio recorder nearby during the session. The audio recorder will turn your table tipping session into an EVP session as well, and the video camera can be stationed at a low angle to make sure that nobody was using their legs to move the table during the session.

4. Use an EMF detector on the table. Since any genuine movement of the table will be done by a spirit in close proximity, placing an EMF detector on the table is a good way to verify that presence. If the table begins moving and the EMF detector is going off, that's a great way to back up an event with some data.

5. Keep the session light and positive. Attitude and intentions go a long way with drumming up the energy spirits require to perform work. If you're having fun and everyone is projecting a bit of positive energy, you may find yourself getting great results.

Right up there with table tipping is the use of a pendulum. This is another old-school technique for speaking to spirits and, if done correctly, can actually be quite effective. You can couple the pendulum up with your table tipping session by simply placing it in the center of the table and prompting the spirit to move the pendulum vs. the table. You can also use the pendulum by itself. But what is a pendulum?

Essentially, a pendulum is an object suspended from a string. Ideally, it should be attached to a stand so that you can place it on a sturdy surface. A lot of pendulums must be held by a person's hand, which can cause a lot of false movement on the part of the holder. To avoid any trickery or inadvertent movement, always tie the pendulum to a stand. Pendulums are often sold with a stand, but you can also hang it from a small easel or another nearby object. Many avid users of pendulums believe the use of a crystal as your pendulum object can provide better results. This could be true. Using a pendulum object that can conduct electromagnetic energy makes logical sense, and certainly can't hurt. Crystals or light, metal objects would provide this type of conductivity.

Take precautions to avoid anything magnetic that's near your pendulum and to use a video camera while performing a pendulum session. This will prevent anyone from possibly blowing toward the pendulum or otherwise skewing the results. To use it properly, you will want to first ask any spirit present to indicate how he or she wants to answer questions. First say, "Please indicate what 'yes' will be." Hopefully, the pendulum will make a movement either side-to-side or circular (clockwise or counterclockwise). Then ask for a "no" indicator. Once the answers are clarified, you can then begin asking questions.

Some investigators also use a technique known as "automatic writing." The problem with this approach is that you are relying on the spirit to operate through a person to write on a piece of paper. This is almost like "channeling" a ghost like a medium. Since there's no way to know if a spirit is actually manipulating the pencil—and it's not just the writer faking it—this is not the most practical way of interacting with an entity.

Of course, the easiest method for participation is to employ a few trigger objects. These are lightweight objects ghosts can move around to indicate their presence. Placing a trigger object in front of a camera, then asking any spirit to move it, is a simple way to get something going and to document that activity. As with the table tipping method, there are some simple steps you should take to maximize this opportunity:

1. Use something light but stationary. Most investigators that I've seen in the field employing a trigger object use a ball. The problem is that a ball moves way too easily without any help from anything paranormal. A slight draft, even the type associated with a person passing by, can move a light ball—not to mention the fact that many surfaces can be uneven without noticing it. I use small Styrofoam cones that florists put fake flowers in for our trigger experiments. They are light, but not susceptible to the problems mentioned here.

2. If possible, use an object that's pertinent to the location. Even though you cannot know for sure who a ghost may be, you may at least have a good suspicion. Let's say witnesses have often seen the spirit of a little girl; little girls like dolls. Using something a little girl would like may provide better results than the standard trigger object.

3. Employ a motion detector and/or an EMF detector along with the trigger object. Once you've placed your object in a spot, try putting an EMF detector nearby that has an audible alarm. If something starts happening, the detector can alert you. A motion detector can do the same thing—just make sure the trigger object is where you want it before turning on the motion detector. The

beauty of using this technique is that you will be alerted if there is ANY movement of the object at all (paranormal or not). This may assist you with debunking any claims of objects moving.

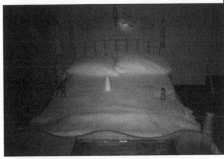

Typical trigger object setup with motion detectors. Courtesy of Paranormal Inc.

A great way to employ a pendulum in a controlled manner is to create what's been dubbed by the paranormal world as an Irish Wind Chime. *This means taking a small set of wind chimes that are on a stand and covering it with a large glass bowl or hurricane used for candles. By doing this, you remove the possibility of any wind moving the chimes and you increase the odds that any activity is of a paranormal nature.*

Instigators

While table tipping, using a pendulum, and employing trigger objects can generally be accepted by most everyone working in the field of parapsychology, there are also a few techniques out there that bring an amount of controversy along with them. I call these types of approaches/devices "instigators." Not only do they instigate debate when they are used, but when they are approached in a neutral manner, they can often instigate spiritual activity.

Perhaps the most well known instigator is the Ouija board. Also known as a "talking" or "oracle" board, this is another device that hails back to the Spiritualists, and up until the release of the movie *The Exorcist*, it was generally considered a benevolent thing. Today, talking boards are extremely polarizing and can spawn hours of debate among investigators. Some believe the Ouija to be evil or even demonic in nature, while others have no such reservations about them. The reality is that ANY object is benevolent until it is used in a negative way.

When we look at the Ouija debate, it has striking similarities to the gun control debate. Is a gun, in itself, evil? No. I think we can all agree with that. It is, simply, a gun. Can a gun be used to do bad things? Absolutely. But the police also use guns to defend our communities, so they can also be good things. Apply this line of thought now to a Ouija board. To me, it is absurd to think a game that's manufactured by Hasbro or Parker Brothers is inherently evil. What's more important is how a spirit may think about it …

Let me elaborate. Let's pretend you are a person who passed away in the early 1900s. While you were alive, you would have been at least aware of the Spiritualist movement and, most likely, things like Ouija boards and séances. Now here you are haunting your old house and you see a visitor (you, the investigator) pulling out a Ouija board. Because of what you know, you may have an underlying belief that a Ouija board WORKS. This in turn may instigate you to respond when the Ouija board is used.

Since, like a gun, a Ouija board will be used however you intend it to be used, I have no problem with them. As long as you keep a positive attitude and keep the line of questioning light (focusing on what spirits did while alive vs. how they died, etc.) you will have no problems with a talking board.

Examples of other instigators include the use of tarot cards, "magic candles," and incense. Basically, if an object has an occult or religious connotation, it can be used as an instigator. I know, I know … I just said "religious." The same scenario I mentioned above about the Ouija board could be applied equally well to religious objects. If a spirit was religious while alive, he or she is probably still going to respond to religious articles. Remember, the goal here is to get some interaction going with the ghosts. So it may take something like an instigator to make this happen.

Historic Case—
The Exorcist Case

As I mentioned earlier, the bad reputation of the Ouija board primarily comes from the movie (and book of the same name) *The Exorcist*. In the movie, a young girl would become possessed after playing with a Ouija board by herself in the basement of her house. Her conversations with a spirit dubbed Mr. Howdy would lead to the devil possessing her and a battle between good and evil. After this movie hit theaters, reports of possessions would skyrocket worldwide, much to the dismay of the clergy. Another side effect would be a negative attitude concerning the use of Ouija boards.

Not only would they now be regarded as a "doorway" to demonic infestation and possession, but a whole host of myths would be introduced—such as playing with a board by yourself is more dangerous than playing with a group of people. There are, today, numerous such superstitions about talking boards. It is interesting to note, though, that the real life exorcism case that author Peter Blatty based his book upon had very little to do with a Ouija board.

Author Thomas B. Allen documented the real life case featured in Blatty's book in his tome, *Possessed*. The real case involved a young boy who local clergy in Maryland believed to be possessed. The boy would go on to a Jesuit institution in St. Louis, Missouri, where a series of exorcisms were performed at several locations before he would be "free" of demonic influence. Today, long after the exorcism of the boy in St. Louis, there are a lot of opinions concerning this case. Many believe the exorcism was an extreme overreaction to what was most likely a simple haunting/poltergeist.

Of course, nobody knows the truth of events that took place except the clergy and the young boy. One thing is certain, though, the Ouija had little-to-nothing to do with the case other than the boy is said to have liked playing with one of the boards with his aunt when she was still alive. For those who subscribe to the theory that the boy was haunted, it is the aunt who is thought to be the ghost that plagued him. Maybe if they had used a

Ouija board while helping the young boy, it would have instigated the aunt's ghost to appear and we would never have had one of the best horror movies of all time…

DICE—Capture

When you examine the four elements of DICE, it's better to think of them as one system rather than a series of events. I say this because throughout any investigation, you are constantly trying to capture evidence—just as you are always trying to detect activity and trying to get it to escalate. In a way, the four parts of DICE work together. Of course, all is for naught if you don't actually capture any evidence.

Since the specifics of capturing audio, video, and photographic evidence during an investigation have already been covered in their respective chapters, I want to talk about additional ways you can capture proof of a haunting—and how you can assist your investigation with the capture of evidence.

Throughout this book, there are sidebars that lay out various low-tech solutions to ghost hunting; these should not be overlooked. You will be limited by how many video cameras and audio recorders you have, so using low-tech items can be a great way to get evidence of activity without dedicating a camera/recorder to that spot. For instance, you may station your two video cameras in the two hottest spots of a paranormal location; in other areas where you don't have a camera, you can try the flour trick mentioned in the sidebar here, use Irish Wind Chimes, or another method. If something happens while using one of the low-tech techniques,

Long before ghost hunters became depen- dent upon electronic gear, there were lots of low tech ways to document paranormal activity.

One such way was the use of flour or talcum powder. A commonly reported type of activity is the sound of footsteps. To test whether this is just a sound, or if there are actual ghostly feet hit- ting the floor, you can sprinkle some flour/ powder on the floor and then take a look for footprints after you hear their sounds.

you can then take photos of the event with a camera.

There are other things you can do to sort of "prime the environ- ment" to capture paranormal activi- ty as well. One is to make sure you are supplying ample electromagnetic energy. Some devices give off rather large amounts of this naturally—and keeping these devices plugged in is one way you can help escalate the activity in a haunted place.

DICE—Escalate

Some examples of equipment that emit strong EMFs include alarm clocks, microwave ovens (even when they aren't running), and lamps. Test these types of items using your EMF detector; if you identify a few of these things, you can consider mov- ing them to another spot within a location to pump energy into the environment. Of course, a quick online search will also bring you paranormal tech providers that make units designed to create a strong electromagnetic field for this pur- pose as well. Making sure there are ample EMFs in the environment is one way to help escalate activity in a haunted location.

Since it takes more and more energy for an entity to consistently perform actions throughout an investigation, you will need more than just EMFs introduced into the air. The best tool for this is you, the investigator.

Call it an aura, bio-energy, or whatever you like, but personal experience has proven to me that the more you interact with a spirit, the more activity happens. And if you can keep the cycle of detection, interaction, and capturing going, paranormal activity will continue to escalate. When you first kick off an investigation, you may only capture a few EVPs (and you won't know about these until later) or the typical sounds associated with a ghost/haunting. But as you keep working with the spirit(s) present, you will notice that the activity will get bigger and more pronounced. Examples of this may include objects moving, hearing disembodied voices, or even experiencing the sensation of being touched.

If you're lucky, all of your hard work may even culminate in the appearance of an apparition. If you're lucky. This phenomenon is not nearly as common as television makes it appear, though. You should attempt to do this interaction using positive energy first; if this doesn't work, you can always turn to provocation and become a living instigator. But once you go down the road of insults and demanding action, it's hard to go back to being "good cop." You would be surprised how far a little sympathy can go during an investigation anyway. After all, it's hard being a ghost!

Trigger Phrases

As I have mentioned before, it's always better to enter an investigation with the assumption that you're dealing with an intelligent spirit. So let's assume that this is the case and you are dealing with an entity that is actively watching and listening to everything you do within his or her environment. With that being the case, it doesn't really make sense for one investigator to look at another and to say something like, "Well, let's try provoking the spirit into doing something." Wouldn't a ghost hear this and possibly decide to ignore your attempts?

Instead of stating your intent during an investigation, try using a set of simple "trigger phrases" to set up a new investigative approach. If you're tired of being a nice guy during a case, you can say something like, "I don't think any spirit in this house wants to play along with us." This will serve as a cue for your fellow investigators to switch gears into a more aggressive, provoking style of investigating. Similar phrases can be used to go a more sympathetic route or to even bring something to the attention of your group.

For instance, let's say you actually find yourself in the middle of something that's looking more and more like a religious case or that you find evidence of trickery. You can create a trigger phrase that will cue everyone to rally outside the location at a vehicle or another safe spot to discuss the situation.

Ghost Story— The Deason House

During the shooting of the documentary *Ghosts of War,* I would visit many haunted sites associated with the American Civil War. One of these sites, the Deason House, is located in southern Mississippi and is known to be haunted after serving as an impromptu hospital for wounded soldiers. In addition to reputedly housing a historic spirit, there are also accounts that include the apparitions of past family members who once lived in the premises.

Over the course of our investigation at this house, we managed to detect and interact with an entity we believed to be the ghost of a young girl. For over half an hour, I personally played a game of hide-and-seek with this spirit. I would use an analog EMF detector to search for the spirit, and then when the meter began to go off, I would say, "I found you!" Upon saying this, the EMF detector would immediately go completely flat—as if the ghost ran away to hide again. This was repeated over and over again before I told the spirit that the game was over.

After a review of the audio from this location, I had a startling discovery: the entire time we played hide-and-seek, the spirit of the young girl was speaking to us! And as the game progressed, and we interacted with the ghost more and more, the voice got louder and more frequent. At one point, while searching for the girl, I said, "Where are you?" I was rewarded with a "yoo hoo" from the girl. At another point the girl directed us to "turn around." And after I had ended our game, there was a frustrated sigh and an EVP of the girl saying, "Can you do it again?" This is just one example of how inter-action can escalate activity during an investigation.

So now you know how to use your gear and how to conduct a viable paranormal investigation. What's next? For some, knowing the tools of the trade is enough to get out there and wrangle up that first investigation. For others, though, this may be the first major step involved with setting up their own paranormal group or organization.

Creating a
Paranormal Group

*There is a definite excitement in learning about a fresh
haunting, for there is always the possibility that this venture into the unknown may bring a never-to-be-forgotten
experience, or better still, that this may be the spontaneous
phenomenon that will prove for all time the objective reality of such activity.*

—Peter Underwood (A Host of Hauntings, *1973*)

Before you task yourself with setting up a paranormal organization, you should first ask yourself IF you
should set one up! What, exactly, do you want to achieve
and/or experience from the world of the paranormal? If you
simply have an interest in ghosts and hauntings, you might
consider going it alone or with a close friend. After all, the
bulk of the haunted locations at your disposal will be public
places like restaurants, hotels, bed and breakfasts, parks, and
museums, so there will always be other customers around
for your safety.

If, however, your goal is proof of the afterlife or the
expansion of the field of parapsychology, the work involved
with such a venture may require more than one investigator

at any given time. Other reasons for wanting co-investigators may include wanting camaraderie or to create a new social network for meeting others like yourself. In either case, this will mean joining an existing paranormal group (something you should not overlook—oftentimes, established groups are well connected with haunted locations and have sizable amounts of gear at their disposal) or creating a new group.

Joining a local paranormal investigation team may be as simple as an online search and a quick e-mail. These days, there are often multiple groups in larger cities, so chances are there's at least one near you. Paranormal organizations will always have a "contact us" link on their webpage (mostly so they can be contacted in the event of a haunting), so use that to voice your desire to join their organization and, hopefully, you will be admitted.

If there are no paranormal groups in your area or the views of the existing groups do not coincide with your own (sometimes a key consideration), you may have to create your own group.

Decisions and Direction

When creating a new group, the decisions you make early on will affect you for as long as that group exists. So choose carefully! Considerations include the direction or style of the group, how formal the group will be, and the goals of the group. Let's take a look at each of these.

There are three basic types of paranormal groups: Science, Psi, and Religious. Sometimes a group will be a combination of these types—at least to an extent. This usually means that group employs psychics or adheres to a religious code, but will use scientific-based gear to gather evidence. This can be a conflict of interest in some cases, but if you are able to balance your own beliefs while still sticking to a scientific method, more power to you! Whichever type of group you create, you will want to specifically mention this in your mission statement. That way, you will only attract investigators of a like mind—or at least avoid those who refuse to work the same way as you.

Psi Groups

If you make the decision to use psychics, remember that they are not all the same; there are quite a few different types. There are full-fledged psychics who believe they can either predict the future and/or reveal the past. Then there are "sensitives" or "intuits" who simply believe they have more of an insight into the paranormal than the average Joe or that they have the ability to detect spirits. The last category of psychic you may encounter is the rarest and is known as a "medium." These psychics claim to be able to channel spirits through their own body and can allow them to speak for themselves.

Since there is no way to actually ever know if a psychic is authentic or not, you should know that there are some tests you can run on people who claim to have this gift. These include the Dice Test (in which a person attempts to either predict the amount of sixes that will turn up in thirty throws or they actually try to influence the dice to come up with a six), the use of Zener cards (cards with emblems on them that a person attempts to predict), or you can simply take the person to an undisclosed location (that you have a lot of information about) and see what the self-proclaimed psychic can tell you. In this case, take great care to not give away any information in advance; it's amazing how much information you can come up with after you've had a minute or two on Google (even through a cell phone).

The bottom line is that true psychics are a rare breed—and even those who manage to convince us of their authenticity are often exposed as charlatans. So be careful allowing such a person to guide your group or investigation. We are all blessed with instinct and intuition, and using that is perfectly acceptable to a degree. But also keep this in mind: no client will ever want all the evidence of their haunting coming from a psychic!

Religious Groups

It should also be noted that there are pitfalls to being a religious paranormal group. Besides the fact that religion and the paranormal often contradict one another (many religions do not support the belief of ghosts), you will always be working within somebody else's environment. And when you are in someone else's business or home, it is important to respect their wishes and beliefs. So if they are Jewish, they probably will not look too kindly on you throwing around the name of Jesus in their home!

Religion is a personal thing and you can allow it to guide your own actions, but it should not be confused with researching and investigating the paranormal. After all, are you proving the existence of ghosts, or of God?

Science-Based Group

Having the inherent neutrality of a science-based group can be a huge plus. Since you are not pushing any religion or psychic visions on the client, they can be assured that any opinions you formulate concerning their location are based on fact and evidence gathered during an investigation. Going this route also means you can spend your valuable time at a location concentrating on getting footage and data rather than following false leads and/or using controversial techniques.

If you decide to go the scientific way, you will also attract a more serious style of investigator. Oftentimes, fans of the paranormal decide to "become" a psychic or demonologist because they like being the center of attention during an investigation—or they have a flair for the dramatic. Neither of these will serve you very well during an investigation. Serious parapsychologists divorce themselves from the concepts of good and evil and approach cases with a neutral mindset. As I mentioned earlier, any event can be viewed as good or bad. For instance, if a spirit touches a person in a home, how you react to that event will decide what you think about it. If the person panics, the event may be looked at as menacing or evil. While if that person is calm, he or she may just think the ghost is trying to get some attention.

Science-based paranormal groups typically focus on using scientific gear (such as the equipment mentioned in the previous chapters) and using sound investigative techniques to tackle a haunting. Employing the scientific method means that we make observations during a case, we formulate hypotheses concerning the activity that's occurring, and then we test them. And when we capture evidence of this activity to back up these hypotheses, it's all the better!

Once you've decided on the type of group you are creating, you should also determine just how formal your group is going to be. There is nothing wrong with starting up an informal group on Meetup.com or Yahoo Groups and simply getting together once a month to share locations, knowledge, and occasionally ghost hunt. This is an easy route and requires little effort on your part. But you may be interested in having that cool website and displaying your evidence for the world to see, right?

Getting Your Group Together

Creating a more formal group means having an online presence and opening yourself up to others in the paranormal field. It's no big secret that squabbles between paranormal groups is common—especially when there are multiple groups within one area. It's a sad affair, but a truth nonetheless. There are people out there who simply look upon everyone else as competition and they will stoop to incredible lows to bait you into arguments and feuds. These groups are to be avoided and ignored. If you do not respond to them, they will eventually go away. It has been my experience that these groups become known for their negative attitudes and methods and usually do a good job of ostracizing themselves from the paranormal community.

But this is one of the challenges of being a formal paranormal group—along with the extra work involved with maintaining a website, setting up more structured investigations, and responding to requests for help. It should also be noted that even though you may be a formal or "professional" group, it is an industry standard that no paranormal organization ever charges a client for an investigation. This means that everything you do will be financed by your own pocketbook! Suddenly that informal Yahoo Group doesn't look so bad, right?

Once you know what style of group you want to create and how formally it will be constructed, you will then have to determine your goals. These, too, should be spelled out in your group's mission statement so there is no confusion among members. If your goal is to have a good time and to simply visit haunted places, make that known so more serious ghost hunters can do something different. And if you have a loftier goal, then that should be stated so you can avoid thrill-seekers and those who are unwilling to actually learn how to ghost hunt properly.

Finding the right people to investigate with you can mean the difference between enjoying your ghostly adventures and struggling to keep your tongue in check. Since so much of what we do in an investigation is based upon observation, it's important that we trust every single person we take into a haunted place. If you cannot take what a person is telling you as the truth, then that person should probably not be in your group.

Recreational vs. Professional

The division between recreational ghost hunting vs. professional ghost hunting is huge. To individual parapsychologists, it is a matter of choice that is of great import. The decision to be a professional investigator brings a lot of responsibility, as well as a set of expectations that cannot be ignored. If you are simply interested in indulging your desire to visit haunted places and ghost hunt (and there's nothing wrong with that), then avoid private cases and don't worry about setting up a website (unless it's just a blog for you to write about your own experiences).

Of course, before you get online, you will want to choose a name for your group. Most opt for a name that represents a certain area. Choose your name wisely. People will associate you with your name. If you say you are the "Memphis Ghost Chasers," folks will think you only investigate Memphis and the surrounding area. With so many geographic locations now taken by other investigators, a lot of paranormal groups go with a more neutral name (such as my group, Paranormal Inc.). The beauty of this is that you may get contacted by people from all over the world!

Another consideration is the use of any "ghost words" in your group's name. If you put a word like ghost or haunting in your name, people will only associate your group with that phenomenon. This is fine if you are only interested in researching ghosts. If, however, you plan to branch out into other areas of the unknown (such as ufology or cryptozoology), then you may want to stick to a name that's based around words like "paranormal" and "phenomenon." Once you have decided on your group's name, you can then worry about nailing down that domain name for your website and getting online.

Once your website is up and you've declared your group open for business, you instantly become a professional group—and clients who contact you will expect a certain amount of knowledge, experience, and results. The key word here is *results*. Results may simply mean answering some of the questions a client may have about the activity they are experiencing, but it can also mean bringing some sort of resolution to a case that will sufficiently allow the client to feel comfortable in their own environment. Remember, your goal as an investigator is twofold: evidence and peace of mind for the client.

A good thing for professional groups to do is to keep a few local clergy on call. Contact them and introduce yourself, then explain that you are not clergy yourself and that you want to be able to call upon them for house blessings, family counseling, or other religion-specific tasks. Chances are you can meet at least one member of a church willing to help you out. And oftentimes, a blessing and some counseling is all a family may need if they are looking for anything religious. This also extricates you from performing religious rituals you may be unfamiliar with.

Other types of resolution may involve debunking common household problems (which may mean calling upon a plumber or electrician), explaining to the client that any entities present are harmless, or suggesting a qualified psychologist/psychiatrist for counseling (which can be especially true of situations where children may be psychologically scarred from activity occurring around them). Most often, these are the methods you will use to reassure a client and to bring about some form of resolution.

Of course, if you are a strictly recreational group, you will stick to more public haunted places, like the aforementioned restaurants, B&Bs, and hotels, so you will not have to worry about the psychological impact of your investigation upon inhabitants. Instead, you will have the thrill of the ghost hunt and the review that follows it.

Historic Case—
The Borley Rectory

Over the course of his illustrious career, paranormal investigator Harry Price would visit a lot of interesting places. One of the most memorable of his cases was the infamous Borley Rectory.

Located in Essex county of England, Borley Rectory was constructed in 1863 by Reverend Dawson Ellis Bull. In 1900, one of the reverend's daughters, a girl named Ethel, claimed to see the apparitions of a nun and a priest on the property. According to the family, the building resided on the site of a thirteenth-century monastery and it was presumed that these spirits were associated with that place.

Harry Price would investigate the haunting of the rectory between the years of 1929 and 1938 and would even write a book about his experiences called *The Most Haunted House in England*. Price claimed to have witnessed numerous paranormal events at the site—events that would span the residence of several different families in the rectory.

After his death in 1948, however, the English paranormal community would dissect and discredit almost everything associated with Price's investigation. Allegations of faking activity and affecting the environment of the rectory (an accusation supported by at least one inhabitant of the property) would also emerge.

Today, the case is hotly debated. Was the Borley Rectory haunted? According to many of the past inhabitants, it most certainly was. So how could an investigator as highly regarded as Price be so criticized for his findings? This is the nature of the paranormal field. Regardless of the quality of evidence you find, you will always encounter those who disagree with your findings. Being prepared for controversy and debate is just one of the things to expect when you post your findings online.

Of course, there are other pitfalls as well …

Avoiding the Demonic

Again, this is the realm of religion. If you are notified of a case that has "demonic" qualities or the client simply believes that they are currently being infested by demons, take a close look at the facts before accepting or declining the investigation. Separate what the client is saying from what is actually happening at the home; if the symptoms of the case point to a haunting instead of demonic infestation, then you may want to take the case. You can do this type of client a lot of good by helping them realize they have a simple haunting instead of something more nefarious.

If, on the other hand, it does sound like a religious case, inform the client that they should probably contact their local clergy. If they don't belong to any church, you can always call upon your own contacts to help them out in this regard.

Sometimes symptoms of a negative entity or demonic infestation can even be mundane things at a location. For instance, if somebody reports experiencing a sickening feeling in a particular area, you may want to do a thorough sweep with an EMF detector. People can actually be hypersensitive to electromagnetic fields—an affliction that can make people sick to their stomachs, have headaches, and even hallucinate (if the field is strong enough). However, people can also be similarly affected by things like natural-gas leaks and high barometric pressure.

Ghost Story— Private Case in Mississippi

One of the strangest cases I have ever investigated involved a woman who lived way out in the country in the state of Mississippi. The case was being investigated by another paranormal group—friends of mine—who found themselves confronting a variety of different types of paranormal activity. According to the owner of the property, the residents were plagued by an evil presence that would throw objects, emit horrible smells, and even once possessed a person (an act witnessed by my friends).

After questioning the other investigators, I quickly realized that most of the reported activity fell under the heading of "normal haunting." However, because the residents did feel like they were under demonic assault, there was a high degree of panic and anxiety in the home that was influencing everyone present. I was convinced that it was this air of hysteria that was prompting one male in the home to think he was being possessed.

Once I visited the location for myself, and performed a rather lengthy investigation, I was able to determine that the family was, indeed, experiencing a haunting. They were simply frightened about the whole affair and watching entirely too many horror movies about the devil, possessions, etc. When I sat down with the client and showed her the evidence I had gathered (several EVPs and photos), I was able to reassure her that the place was simply haunted and that there were ways she could cope with this situation.

I would end up calling in a member of the Unitarian Church that I know in the area to perform a blessing on the home, and I left the client feeling much better about the situation there. Ironically, she eventually ended up moving away from the home with her family. She simply could not take living in a haunted place. Sometimes this will be the case, and moving away may be the only resolution that satisfies the client.

How to Get Online

Depending on whether you want to be a recreational group or a professional group, you will have to decide if you want to create a website. Professionals definitely need a website if they want to be noticed in their community. Recreational ghost hunters don't need a site at all, although it is fun for ghost hunters to create a free blog and to write about their adventures. This is also a great way to document your investigations for your own use. (Consider it free online archiving.)

To create a website, you will first want to decide what your domain name (www.whatever …) is going to be and to choose a domain host. A quick online search will give you tons of hosts—and these hosts will have tools that will allow you to figure out if your domain name is available. Once you have chosen a name and a host, you will then have to determine what level of website will serve you best. Most hosts have simple drag-and-drop style website editors that will allow you to construct your site with photos, text, links, etc. And there will be several different plans for you to choose from (single-page site, multiple-page sites, and other options). Just keep in mind that the bigger your site is, the more money it may cost per month to maintain it through a host.

Our site (www.paranormalincorporated.com) is actually a blog with a registered domain name. Since we chose to go the blog route, we don't have to pay a monthly fee to maintain our website; instead, it is up to one of our members to keep the site up to date and to periodically add new content. I highly recommend going this route since it is one of the cheapest ways to have a website, and it allows you to change anything on the site whenever you want instead of relying on a webmaster to do the upkeep.

Since you will probably want to post your findings on your website as well (when the client has given you permission to do so), you may also need to find an online host for any photos, audio, or video you capture during your investigation. There are many free options: we use Photobucket for photos, Alonetone for audio clips, and our Facebook account for video clips (once you upload videos to Facebook, select the "embed" option to place it on your website). Once again, though, a blog will typically allow you to attach photos or video clips to your posts.

In addition to your website, you may also decide to get your group on social networking sites like Twitter, Facebook, or MySpace. This is perfectly fine; just link to these additional pages and make sure to update them regularly to keep them relevant. They can be great tools for networking with other paranormal groups and for recruiting potential new members. A lot of groups also opt to add "forums" or "message boards" to their websites for visitors to chime in on subjects, findings, and events. These can be great for drumming up cases and sharing knowledge with others in the field.

Maintaining Your Group

Depending on the size of your paranormal group, meetings may be as simple as making a few phone calls and getting together. In other cases, you may have to carefully schedule meetings so that members can plan in advance for them. This is especially true if your group has a lot of members. Either way, meetings are important. It is there that you will introduce new members, discuss upcoming events/cases, and generally share information.

As mentioned earlier, members are also important in that they can contribute gear to the group. Since you will not be earning any money by performing investigations, anything you use while investigating will be purchased by the investigators. Of course, you can also earn revenue for purchasing new equipment in other ways ...

You can sell T-shirts, hats, and other merchandise with your group's name/logo on them. You can set up events (like classes on ghost hunting) to make money, and you

Café Press (www.cafepress .com) is a great online source for designing and selling gear. *It costs you nothing to set up an online store that you can promote on your website and it makes it easy to create T-shirts, hats, and numerous other types of products.*

might even find yourself writing a book about the paranormal at some point (imagine that!). These are all great ways to slowly build up a pool of money to buy your wish-list gear like that super-expensive thermal-imaging camera.

Another great way to sell gear, as well as to get your group more local attention, is to get the press involved. Whenever you get a case that is more public-oriented and open to publicity (such as a haunted hotel, museum, or similar public location), consider inviting a local reporter along on your investigation. Not only will you get your group in the paper/on television, but you will also provide publicity for the location. This often will get you in their good graces—especially if they are promoting their haunting in any way (such as hosting ghost tours and Halloween events).

Once you have performed a few investigations and have gained some practical experience in the field, you can contact a paranormal radio show about appearing on their program. Some are well-known national programs (such as *Coast to Coast*

AM), but there are hundreds of locally operated online radio programs that need content for their shows. You can even get a copy of your interview/appearance and feature that on your website with your other press links and clips.

Of course, all of this depends on you getting some cases under your belt and gaining that valuable experience ghost hunting.

Getting Your First Case

So now you have set up your paranormal group. What's next? Investigating a haunted location, that's what! Whether you have decided to be a professional group or a recreational group, your first case will most likely be at a public place that you set up yourself. Getting a private case is a rare event for any organization—even for those who have been around for a long time with a great online presence.

Have you ever noticed when you browse other paranormal groups' websites that it seems like they go to a lot of cemeteries? Don't be one of these groups! Besides the fact that most cemeteries are not haunted, traipsing around grounds that are considered to be holy to a lot of people can earn you a poor reputation very quickly. Posting stories about cemeteries also encourages less scrupulous thrill-seekers to visit them as well—which can lead to inappropriate behavior, vandalism, and sometimes arrests—not the best way to spread the word about your ghost-hunting group.

Instead of lurking around areas that just "seem" to be scary or haunted, do some research regarding possible haunted spots in your area. Odds are, there will be at least a handful of haunted hotels, restaurants, and similar locations in your vicinity (check out my other book from Llewellyn Publishing, *The Ghost Hunter's Field Guide*—it has state-by-state listings of just such haunted places for you to visit). Investigating a haunted hotel or restaurant may be as simple as having a meal there or renting a room, then mentioning to the staff that you are a ghost hunter. Using this approach has gotten my group numerous investigations in the past.

Finding a haunted place like this may actually be TOO easy these days; paranormal tourism is at an all-time high, so it's quite common to come across a lot of places touting themselves as being haunted. Sometimes this is just a crafty marketing technique, sometimes it is all too true. You will have to do some research to figure out which is the case.

Another great way to get your first investigation, and future investigations, is to meet other paranormal groups and to set up a co-investigation with them. As I mentioned above, there are probably already groups in your area, so introduce yourself and make some friends. Once you show them that you aren't going to be a contentious, resentful group and that you want to meet others in the field, you will be surprised how many people open up to you.

Ghost Story— Magnolia Hill Bed and Breakfast

When I heard that a Helena, Arkansas, bed and breakfast was known for their haunting, I decided that this would be a great opportunity to meet other locals in the paranormal field. So we set up an overnight trip to this location along with two other groups in our area. Since the B&B had six rooms for lodgings, each group got to rent two rooms for their use.

The B&B was extremely grateful for the business and we all had a great time meeting each other, as well as performing an investigation. It was also a prime opportunity to get a look at how other groups were performing investigations.

During such collaborations, sometimes we would learn an entirely new approach to a technique. At others, we got to compare various brands of gear and discuss how effective they are. Everyone involved learned a lot, had a lot of fun, and found an inexpensive way to get another case under their belts.

Wrapping It All Up

Once you have performed your first investigation, and have made a thorough review of your footage, you will have to determine what you can do with your evidence. If your case was on private property, make sure to get permission from the owners if you plan to put anything online for the public to see—and remember that you can always use anonymous names, locations, etc. Putting evidence from your cases on your website is essential for gaining any "street cred" in the paranormal field. Anyone can set up a website declaring themselves ghost hunters; it actually takes a true investigator to put up evidence to back up this claim!

Of course, when you put evidence up on your page, controversy will follow … that's to be expected, so be prepared for it. Not everyone agrees about what is paranormal. All you can do is perform the best investigation you can, attempt to debunk any evidence you gather, and be respect-ful of the location when posting your evidence. If some-body doesn't agree with what you find and post, that's their problem. Just roll with the punches, stick to your investiga-tive guns, and don't get baited into arguments concerning your methods.

If you follow the guidelines and techniques laid out in this book, being a ghost hunter can be a positive and rewarding endeavor. You purchased this book and decided to invest in a lot of gear because you enjoy the subject of the paranormal and want to learn more. Why invest so much time, effort, and money into an endeavor if you're not going to enjoy it?

So get out there and hunt those ghosts!

appendix a

Suggested Gear List

Though this is by no means an all-inclusive list of everything you can use in a paranormal investigation, it should serve as a jumping off point for you. It also covers all the basics you will need for ghost hunting. Using this list is also a great way to make sure you take everything you need to an investigation—and to make sure you leave with it all when you return home!

Basics:

Appropriate clothing

Journal or paper and pen

Computer for review

Quality set of headphones

Equipment cases

Flashlight

First aid kit

Walkie-talkies

Batteries

Multi-tool or small tool kit

Flour/talcum powder

Measuring tape

Chalk or tape

Audio:

Digital audio recorders

External microphones

Audio cables to connect to computer

Spare batteries/AC adapter

AM radio (for ITC)

Video:

Camcorders or DVR system with cameras

Videotapes (if necessary)

Infrared illuminators or video lights

Tripods

External microphones

Spare batteries/AC adapter

Cables to connect to a TV or computer

Cleaning kit

Photography:
Cameras
Filters (IR, neutral density, UV, etc.)
IR illuminator or light/flash
Film stock (if necessary)
Additional memory cards
Spare batteries/AC adapter
Tripods

Environmental Monitoring:
EMF detectors
Digital thermometers
Weather station
Motion detectors
Compass
Geiger counter
Laser grid/pointer
Ion counter/projector
Electromagnetic field generator

Miscellaneous Gear:
Trigger objects
Instigators (pendulum, Ouija boards, etc.)
Dowsing rods

Investigation
Step-by-Step

This is a cheat sheet of your workflow during an investigation. You can make copies of this page to put in your investigation journal to make sure you perform all the necessary steps during a case.

Pre-Investigation:
Do research
Plan logistics (route, vehicles needed, etc.)
Perform equipment maintenance and inventory
Assemble your team
Perform interviews
Do a walkthrough
Choose a rally point

Investigation—Detect:
Deploy equipment strategically
Perform a vigil
Use motion detectors
Use EMF detectors
Use Geiger counters/ion counters
Use digital thermometers/weather stations

Investigation—Interact:
Perform EVP sessions
Perform ITC sessions
Perform table tipping session
Use trigger objects

Investigation—Capture:
Use photography
Use video cameras
Use audio recorders

Investigation—Escalate:
Use electromagnetic field generators
Use instigators
Try Singapore Theory
Perform a live EVP session
Use ion projectors
Try provoking techniques

Post-Investigation:

Inventory your gear before leaving investigation

Document personal experiences

Upload footage to computer

Review footage and environmental data

Enhance or improve evidence

Prepare an investigation report

Return to location if possible (for debunking)

Share evidence with client

Post results (if permitted to do so by client)

Books:

Allen, Thomas B. *Possessed*. Lincoln, NE: iUniverse.com, Inc., 2000.

Anson, Jay. *The Amityville Horror*. Engelwood Cliffs, NJ: Prentice-Hall Inc., 1977.

Balzano, Christopher. *Ghostly Adventures*. New York: Fall River Press, 2009.

Blatty, Peter William. *The Exorcist*. New York: Harper Torch, 1994.

Carrington, Hereward, and Nandor Fodor. *Haunted People: The Story of the Poltergeist Down Through the Centuries*. New York: Dutton, 1951.

Crowe, Catherine. *The Night Side of Nature: An Investigation of the Paranormal and the Unexplained.* Ware, Hertfordshire, UK: Wordsworth Editions, 2001.

Curran, Robert. *The Haunted.* New York: St. Martin's Press, 1988.

De Felitta, Frank. *The Entity.* New York: G. P. Putnam's Sons, 1978.

Fort, Charles. *Wild Talents.* Radford, VA: Wilder Publications, 2009.

Francis-Cheung, Theresa. *The Element Encyclopedia of the Psychic World: the Ultimate A-Z of Spirits, Mysteries, and the Paranormal.* London: Harper Element, 2006.

Hawes, Jason, and Grant Wilson with Michael Jan Friedman. *Seeking Spirits.* New York: Pocket Books, 2009.

Keel, John. *Operation Trojan Horse.* Lilburn, GA: IllumiNet Press, 1996.

Myers, Arthur. *The Ghostly Register.* Chicago: Contemporary Books, Inc., 1986.

Newman, Rich. *The Ghost Hunter's Field Guide.* Woodbury, MN: Llewellyn Publishing, 2011.

Playfair, Guy Lyon. *The Indefinite Boundary: An Investigation into the Relationship Between Matter and Spirit.* New York: St. Martin's Press, 1976.

Taylor, Troy. *Ghost Hunter's Guidebook.* Decatur, IL: Whitechapel Press, 2007.

Tolstoy, Leo. *Anna Karenina*. Mineola, NY: Dover Publications, 2004.

Underwood, Peter. *A Host of Hauntings: A Shuddersome Book of Ghosts and Ghostly Adventures*. London: Frewin Press, 1973.

Websites:

American Hauntings, www.prairieghosts.com
Audacity Sound Editor, http://audacity.sourceforge.net
Blogger, www.blogger.com
Café Press, www.cafepress.com
Digital Dowsing, www.digitaldowsing.com
Facebook, www.facebook.com
Ghost Village, www.ghostvillage.com
Gimp Photo Editor, www.gimp.org
Meetup, www.meetup.com
MySpace, www.myspace.com
Paranormal Inc., www.paranormalincorporated.com
Twitter, www.twitter.com
Wax Video Editor, www.debugmode.com
Wikimedia Commons, http://commons.wikimedia.org
World ITC, www.worlditc.org
Zwei-Stein Video Editor, www.thugsatbay.com

Alternate Reality Theory—The concept of multiple planes of existence that can sometimes intrude upon us in this world. Thought to possibly be the reason people experience glimpses into the past and, sometimes, residual hauntings.

Apparition—The spectral spirit of a person who was once living. This is the visual version of a ghost.

Barometric Pressure—This is the measure of air pressure in a particular area. Paranormal researchers have documented changes in barometric pressure during a haunting.

Channeling—The process involved with psychics allowing disincarnate spirits to temporarily possess and communicate through them.

Clearing—Process of removing unwanted spirits from a domicile or area. Usually involves candles, incense, etc. rather than the use of religious ritual.

Cold Spot—A self-contained cold area that often appears during a haunting. It's thought that it is caused by a spirit drawing thermal energy from the area.

Cryptozoology—The scientific study of "hidden animals" that are either extinct or yet unproven to exist. Examples of such creatures include the sasquatch, lake monsters, and even recently found "extinct" animals like the coelacanth and thylacine.

Debunk—To disprove an event or validity of a claim. Debunking activity is one of the steps in a thorough paranormal investigation.

Deliverance—The Protestant version of an exorcism. Usually performed by Evangelists in a public setting with much fanfare vs. the use of Roman Ritual as defined by the Catholic Church.

Demon—Non-human spirit thought to perform evil deeds. In some religions it denotes a fallen angel or spirit who now serves the lord of the underworld (Satan, Hades, etc.).

DICE—An acronym for "Detect, Interact, Capture and Escalate." This is the chain of investigation used by the author of this book.

Disembodied Voice—The voice of a spirit that's heard in real time during an investigation. Reports of disembodied voices are commonplace for hauntings.

Dowsing Rods—Also known as "divining rods," these are rods of wood or metal that, reputedly, can lead users to water, ghosts, etc.

DVR—An acronym for "Digital Video Recorder." When coupled with a set of video cameras, a DVR can be used to record video footage during an investigation.

Ectoplasm—A liquid or jelly-like substance that's thought to be left behind after the manifestation of a spirit. Though it's mostly associated with fraudulent acts performed by Spiritualists, the authentic appearance of this substance has been documented.

Elemental—Also known as a nature spirit. This is another type of non-human spirit that can be associated with either good or evil and is usually attributed to an earthly element (fire, water, earth, etc.).

EMF—An acronym for "Electromagnetic Field." This is the natural energy that's given off by electrical appliances, living things, and even magnetic objects like the Earth itself.

Entity—See *Spirit.*

ESP—Acronym for "Extrasensory Perception." This is the ability of psychics to see into the future, the past, etc. Also known as the "sixth sense," it's supposed that all humans have this ability to some degree.

EVP—An acronym for "Electronic Voice Phenomena." A technique for asking questions of the dead and documenting their answers with the use of an audio recorder. The responses recorded are not heard by the questioner during the session but only appear after the fact.

Exorcism—A ritual performed by the Catholic Church to rid a living person of possession by a spirit or demon.

Full Spectrum—The entire range of light that includes visual light, ultraviolet light, and infrared light.

Geiger Counter—A device used to record radioactivity in an area.

Geophone—An instrument that's used to detect movement or tremors in an area. In the paranormal field, geophones are calibrated to pick up the vibrations made by footsteps, movement, etc.

Ghost—The generic term for the appearance of a once living spirit in an environment. This can be as an apparition or in a way that makes their presence known to the living (disembodied voices, moving objects, etc.).

Ghost Light—This is a visible ball of light that's often associated with a haunting, or at least the spirit of someone who has died.

Hagging—The Scandinavian version of sleep paralysis. Though proven to be a natural phenomenon, "hagging" is a legend associated with an evil spirit (succubus/incubus) that actually sits on a living person to paralyze them while they are sleeping.

Haunting—Situation involving a ghost(s) inhabiting a specific area.

Hot Spot—An area known for paranormal activity.

Incubus—An evil, male spirit that's thought to assault women while sleeping. Many consider an incubus to be a form of demon that specializes in nightmares.

Infrared—The portion of the light spectrum that extends beyond the visible color of red. Though it's invisible to the naked eye, objects in this spectrum can be seen with the use of night vision equipment.

Instigator—An object that's used to instigate a reaction from a spirit.

Intelligent (Haunting)—A haunting that involves the spirit of a once living person. Elements of an intelligent haunting include direct responses to queries and the ability to interact with objects and people.

Ions—Positively and negatively charged air particles that are known to affect the environment.

Irish Wind Chimes—A set of normal wind chimes that have been placed under a glass dome. Movement of these chimes can indicate paranormal activity when they are used as a means to interact with a spirit.

ITC—Acronym for "Instrumental Transcommunication." This is the practice of speaking directly to the dead through the use of electronic devices such as radios, televisions, and even computers. Unlike EVP, voices of spirits are heard in real time using this technique.

Live Monitoring Station—Also known as a command center or rally point, this is the spot paranormal investigators station their computer, DVR, gear, etc.

Matrixing—The natural tendency to form recognizable shapes and patterns out of something random. In the realm of the paranormal, this involves seeing "faces" or apparitions in the reflection of glass, etc.

Medium—A specific kind of psychic who has the ability to channel a spirit through his or her body.

Mist—Usually a natural phenomena that is caused by a rapid change in humidity and/or temperature that's often mistaken for paranormal activity.

Orb—Non-paranormal objects that are often captured in photographs and video footage. They are the result of light refracting off airborne dust particles, bugs, etc.

Ouija Board—Also known as a "talking" or "oracle" board, this is a game that involves participants placing their hands on a planchette and asking questions. Responses are spelled out using the letters/numbers written on the board itself.

Paranormal—Literally means "beyond the normal." Generally speaking, it is any event that cannot be explained by conventional science.

Parapsychology—The scientific study of the paranormal.

Pendulum—An object suspended from a piece of string that's often used to interact with a spirit.

Phantom Scents—A scent that is not associated with a particular area and thought to originate from a spirit. The most commonly reported phantom scents include perfume, tobacco smoke, and flowers.

PK—Acronym for "psychokinetic." Term used to describe poltergeist activity or hauntings that are associated with a human agent who may be facilitating the paranormal activity.

Poltergeist—German term for "noisy spirit." A type of haunting that's associated with a human participant—usually unwilling. Characterized by violent movements and profound amounts of activity.

Portal—A weak "veil" that's said to exist between the living world and that of the dead that can often provide the means for a haunting. Such hauntings are thought to often include non-human entities.

Possession—The condition of a spirit inhabiting the body of a living person.

Provocation—The use of negative dialogue and actions in order to get a response from a spirit.

Psychic—A person who has ESP or the ability to perform paranormal acts (telepathy, clairvoyance, etc.).

Rally Point—See *Live Monitoring Station.*

Residual (Haunting)—A type of haunting that does not actually involve a spirit. Thought to be glimpses into an alternate reality or the recording of a specific event into the environment.

Séance—A ritual involving the summoning of a specific spirit and then communicating with that entity. Usually performed by a group of people in a social environment.

Sensitive—A person who exhibits mild extrasensory perception. Usually this involves having "feelings" about an area or sensing the presence of spirits.

Shadow People—A term used by the paranormal community to describe dark, shadow-like apparitions that appear during a haunting.

Singapore Theory—A popular technique used by paranormal investigators that involves playing music from a particular era in order to instigate a response from an entity.

Skeptic—A person with an open mind, though most mistakenly believe a skeptic to be someone who doubts the validity of a phenomenon.

Spirit—Thought to be the discarnate essence that animates a living thing. Also known as a soul.

Spiritualism—A popular movement in the late 1800s and early 1900s that involved communication with the dead through the use of occult objects and séances.

Sprite Lights—A type of paranormal activity that appears as brief sparks of light seen within haunted areas.

Succubus—The female counterpart to the incubus. Also thought by many to be a form of demon, the succubus is said to prey upon men while they are sleeping.

Table Tipping—The non-psychic version of the séance. Involves participants sitting at a table and asking questions of the dead, then getting responses through movement and knocks on the table.

Tagging—The practice of marking events on your audio and video footage, such as when you enter a new room, witness any activity, or make a mundane sound that can be mistaken for the paranormal.

Trigger Object—A physical item that can be manipulated by a spirit.

Trigger Phrase—A key set of words used by investigators to initiate a specific action, such as provocation.

Ufology—The scientific study of UFOs (Unidentified Flying Objects), alien life forms, and alien abduction.

Ultraviolet—A portion of the light spectrum that extends beyond the visible color of violet. Though it is invisible to the human eye, it can be viewed with the use of scientific equipment.

Vigil—A technique used during an investigation that involves investigators remaining still and quiet while observing changes in the environment.

White Noise—A type of randomly generated static within a specific bandwidth that's thought to facilitate communications with the dead.

GET MORE AT LLEWELLYN.COM

Visit us online to browse hundreds of our books and decks, plus sign up to receive our e-newsletters and exclusive online offers.

- • Free tarot readings • Spell-a-Day • Moon phases
- • Recipes, spells, and tips • Blogs • Encyclopedia
- • Author interviews, articles, and upcoming events

GET SOCIAL WITH LLEWELLYN

Find us on
Facebook
www.Facebook.com/LlewellynBooks

Follow us on
twitter™
www.Twitter.com/Llewellynbooks

GET BOOKS AT LLEWELLYN

LLEWELLYN ORDERING INFORMATION

Order online: Visit our website at www.llewellyn.com to select your books and place an order on our secure server.

Order by phone:
- • Call toll free within the U.S. at 1-877-NEW-WRLD (1-877-639-9753)
- • Call toll free within Canada at 1-866-NEW-WRLD (1-866-639-9753)
- • We accept VISA, MasterCard, and American Express

Order by mail:
Send the full price of your order (MN residents add 6.875% sales tax) in U.S. funds, plus postage and handling to: Llewellyn Worldwide, 2143 Wooddale Drive Woodbury, MN 55125-2989

POSTAGE AND HANDLING:
STANDARD: (U.S. & Canada)
(Please allow 12 business days)
$25.00 and under, add $4.00.
$25.01 and over, FREE SHIPPING.

INTERNATIONAL ORDERS (airmail only):
$16.00 for one book, plus $3.00 for each additional book.

Visit us online for more shipping options. Prices subject to change.

FREE CATALOG!

To order, call
1-877-
NEW-WRLD
ext. 8236
or visit our
website

COLIN WILSON

POLTERGEIST

A Classic Study
in Destructive Haunting

Poltergeist
A Classic Study in Destructive Hauntings
COLIN WILSON

Banging noises and disembodied voices coming from nowhere and everywhere at once. Furniture chasing people through the house. Pots and pans and knives and knick-knacks flying through the air. These are the hallmarks of the poltergeist phenomenon.

In this classic book on destructive hauntings, Colin Wilson, renowned authority on the paranormal, examines the evidence and develops a definitive theory of the poltergeist phenomenon. Countless true-life cases of poltergeist infestations have been recorded since the days of ancient Greece. But what are poltergeists? Where do they come from? And why do they appear in our world? From the case of a huge, black-robed monk that terrorized a family for years, to the investigation of a talking mongoose, to true stories of gnomes and demons, this guide explores a fascinating gallery of nasty, noisy entities known as poltergeists.

978-0-7387-1867-5, 384 pp., 6 x 9 $17.95

The Sallie House Haunting
A True Story

DEBRA PICKMAN

Who knew that our experience would push us over the edge of disbelief and through the door of certain terror?

Debra Pickman had always wanted a ghost of her own. She never expected her wish to come horrifically true when she, her husband, and their newborn son moved into a century-old home in Atchison, Kansas, that—to their shock—is also occupied by a fire-starting spirit child named Sallie... and darker, aggressive forces.

Gradually, Debra becomes attached to Sallie and adjusts to her ghostly mischief—toys turning on by themselves, knick-knacks moving, and electrical disruptions. But serious problems arise when she can't control Sallie's habit of lighting fires. What's worse, her husband Tony becomes the victim of scratches, bites, and terrifying ghostly attacks that are clearly the work of other menacing entities. Discover how the ongoing terror takes its toll on their nerves, sanity, and marriage, and what finally forces the Pickmans to flee the infamous Sallie House.

978-0-7387-2128-6, 288 pp., 6 x 9　　　　　　　　**$16.95**

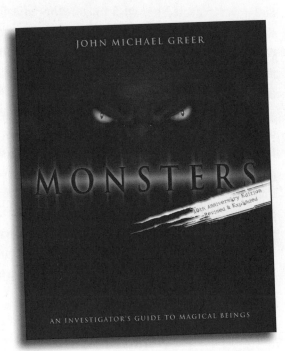

JOHN MICHAEL GREER

MONSTERS

10th Anniversary Edition
Revised & Expanded

AN INVESTIGATOR'S GUIDE TO MAGICAL BEINGS

MONSTERS
An Investigator's Guide to Magical Beings
JOHN MICHAEL GREER

10th Anniversary Edition, Revised and Expanded

Just in time for Halloween, John Michael Greer's mega-popular *Monsters* is now even bigger and better than before! A perennial favorite for both mainstream and magical audiences, this tenth-anniversary edition of the quintessential guide to magical beings features a new preface, new chapters on chimeras and zombies, and updates on werewolves, dragons and the fae.

Join John Michael Greer for a harrowing journey into shadowy realms inhabited by ghosts and aliens, demons and vampires, Old Hags and mermaids. Combining folklore, Western magical philosophy, and actual field experience, *Monsters: An Investigator's Guide to Magical Beings* is required reading for both active and armchair monster hunters.

978-0-7387-0050-2, 336 pp., 7½ x 9⅛ $19.95